D1726457

Media Power and Religions

Manfred L. Pirner
Johannes Lähnemann
(eds.)

Media Power and Religions

The Challenge
Facing Intercultural Dialogue
and Learning

PETER LANG

Frankfurt am Main · Berlin · Bern · Bruxelles · New York · Oxford · Wien

Bibliographic Information published by the Deutsche Nationalbibliothek
The Deutsche Nationalbibliothek lists this publication in the Deutsche Nationalbibliografie; detailed bibliographic data is available in the internet at http://dnb.d-nb.de.

Cover Design:
© Olaf Gloeckler, Atelier Platen, Friedberg

Library of Congress Cataloging-in-Publication Data

Media power and religions : the challenge facing intercultural
    dialogue and learning / Manfred L. Pirner, Johannes Lähne-
    mann (eds.). — 1 [edition].
    pages cm
    ISBN 978-3-631-62537-8
    1. Mass media—Religious aspects. 2. Mass media in religi-
on. 3. Religions. I. Pirner, Manfred L., editor of compilation.
BL638.M423 2013
201'.7—dc23

                                                              2013005173

ISBN 978-3-631-62537-8
© Peter Lang GmbH
Internationaler Verlag der Wissenschaften
Frankfurt am Main 2013
All rights reserved.

Table of Contents

Manfred L. Pirner / Johannes Lähnemann
Introduction 7

SECTON 1: Analyses

Heiner Bielefeldt
Interrelated human rights: the freedom of religion and belief, and the
freedom of opinion and expression 15

Matthias Rohe
Media legislation in Islamic countries 27

Daniel Meier
Looking for the positive: Islam in the media 39

Peter Philipp
Anti-Semitism and Middle Eastern Media 51

Markus A. Weingardt
The presence of religious peace initiatives in the media 65

Norman Richardson
Media and Religious Conflict – Experiences from Northern Ireland 73

SECTION 2: Theological, ethical, and educational perspectives

Jonathan Magonet
The Jewish prohibition of images and modern media culture 87

Saeid Edalatnejad
Pictures, symbols and the media: an Islamic Perspective 97

Johanna Haberer
Media ethics as part of a public theology – a Protestant perspective 107

5

Horst Niesyto
Intercultural education and the media – an educational perspective 117

Manfred L. Pirner
Media culture and interreligious learning – a religious education
perspective 127

Daniel Meier / Peter Philipp
Religion in Journalism: A Proposal for Standards 141

Johannes Lähnemann
Interreligious Textbook Research and Development: A Proposal for
Standards 147

List of Authors 161

Introduction

Manfred L. Pirner & Johannes Lähnemann

There can be no doubt about the high relevance of the public media for the image we have of religion in general and certain religions in particular. News shows on television constantly supply us with pictures of "Islamist terrorism" and convey the impression that religions are mainly sources of conflict in the world, from Northern Ireland or Sudan to Pakistan and the Middle East. The world-wide catastrophic effects of the Muhammad cartoons or the burning of the Qur'an by an American pastor would not have been possible without the world wide web of the internet. Often, the images of religion conveyed by the media seem biased, one-sided or even distorted.

The media have also changed the character of even very traditional religions such as Christianity or Islam. The American "Electronic Churches" seem to find their Muslim counterparts in the popular TV preachers of Arab countries whose mixture of a pragmatic Islam and modern life style apparently appeals to young people. Even a superficial look into history can teach us, though, that media – in a wide sense of the word – have always played an important role for religions and have been prominent subjects of theological and ethical discourse. Since religious realities such as "God" or "a higher world" are not accessible through our human senses, media – e.g. pictures, scriptures or rituals – are needed to symbolize such realities. Also, especially for revelation religions, media are indispensible for passing on the revelation story to the next generation, thus aiming to ignite the same kind of religious experience in them that the original religious community had. The great historical controversies in the Abrahamic religions on the use of images and on the right hermeneutics of holy scriptures show that in the tension between media use and media criticism these religions have over centuries developed a media competence that may also prove helpful for present-day challenges posed by "media culture". Yet, to this very day some religions or religious currents tend to restrict the free expression through, and free circulation of, media and thus come into conflict with basic human rights.

Being aware of all these various links between religions and the media, it seems puzzling that they have rarely found due attention in academic discourse. On the part of media science and media education religions are mostly neglected, and on the part of theory and research on intercultural or interreligious dialogue and learning the significance of the media is neglected.

The present volume aims to address this deficit. Most of its contributions were presented as major papers at an international conference – the 10th Nuremberg Forum – in Nuremberg, Germany, in 2010. Others have been added in order to complement certain aspects. The first section of the book contains analyses of significant intersections of media and religions from the perspectives of various disciplines, mainly philosophical, jurisprudential and journalistic. The second part offers perspectives for a theological understanding of media, for media ethics, media education and religious education; it ends with two proposals for standards for addressing religion(s) in journalism and in school textbook production respectively.

In his opening contribution under *Section 1 (Analyses)* UN Special Rapporteur for the Freedom of Religion and Belief, Professor *Heiner Bielefeldt*, inquires into the *relationship between this human right and the right of freedom of expression.* In the conflicts that frequently arise between the two, many people are inclined to think that they are symptomatic of an insurmountable general antagonism and that one has to decide which of the two is more important in a concrete case, or at least that one has to find some sort of a compromise. Bielefeldt objects to such a view and demonstrates that the various human rights norms themselves are complementary in the sense that they mutually presuppose and mutually reinforce each other: "Whoever wants to support freedom of religion and belief, minority rights and anti-discrimination policies must also, to be credible, be committed to freedom of expression and opinion, and in general to a climate of open discussion. The same is true the other way around in that freedom of expression cannot be defended in a credible way without taking seriously the right to freedom of thought, conscience, religion or belief."

Law professor *Mathias Rohe,* as an expert in Islamic law, offers a substantial overview and analysis of *media legislation in several Islamic countries.* He has to conclude that even today in many parts of the Islamic world freedom of expression and especially freedom of belief are not in good shape, although there are some Muslim scholars and religious leaders who do speak out for these freedoms. In particular Rohe examines the *The Cairo Declaration on Human Rights in Islam* of 1990, *The Arab Charter on Human Rights* of 2004 and the work of Afghan-Malaysian law scholar *Mohammed Hashim Kamali,* one of the few Islamic writers who has expanded on the right of freedom of expression.

The title of *Daniel Meier's* contribution, *Looking for the Positive: Islam in the Media*, clearly indicates the problem he deals with. As a journalist and theologian, Meier draws on content analyses as well as empirical studies to show that the representation of Islam in Western media is not only frequently a distorted one, but also that it is highly controversial: "Evaluating the perception of Islam in the media often bears the hallmarks of a proxy fight between, put simplistically, the critics of Islam and Islam sympathisers." In this fight, it is not easy for journalists to find a way that conforms with their own professional ethos. Meier sketches the criteria that journalists generally use to select and evaluate news material. He concludes by offering helpful ethical as well as practical perspectives.

Peter Philipp has been a journalist with leading German newspapers and radio stations and a long-time correspondent in the Middle East. Based on his rich experience he offers an illuminating analysis of *Anti-Semitism in the Middle Eastern Media*. He shows that anti-Semitism has never been a traditional part of Islam, but rather was imported by Islamic countries from Western and Eastern Christian countries after the founding of the state of Israel – which was the major starting point for anti-Semitic attitudes among the Arab nations. Philipp inquires into the consequences of the Arab spring in this respect, looks back to the implications of the 9/11 experience, analyses the anti-Semitic tendencies in Arab TV stations, and makes it clear that Iran is, to some extent, a special case among the Islamic states of the Middle East in that it distinguishes quite strictly between Jews – who enjoy a considerable degree of freedom inside Iran – and the state of Israel – that is fervently rejected as the satanic ally of the United States.

As indicated above, religions tend to be presented by the media as sources of conflict rather than of peace and reconciliation. *Markus A. Weingardt*, researcher at the Research Institute of the Protestant Academic Association, Heidelberg, and at the World Ethic Foundation in Tübingen, Germany, shows that this is a distorted view of religions. He draws our attention to the numerous *religious peace initiatives* that are mostly neglected by the media. In his book "Religion Macht Frieden" (Religion Makes Peace) Weingardt has collected a whole range of examples from several religions that he draws on in his contribution. He concludes by advancing concrete suggestions for what academics, politicians, religious communities and the media can do to improve the one-sided representation of religions in the media.

Norman Richardson, Head of Teaching & Learning in Religious Studies at Stranmillis University College in Belfast and Secretary of the Northern Ireland Inter-Faith Forum, exemplifies the significance of the relationship between media and religion for the Northern Irish context. In his contribution *Media and Religious Conflict in Northern Ireland* he sketches the challenges this conflict brings for intercultural learning. He vividly describes how media and journalists are in a constant danger of being instrumentalized even against their will, which makes journalistic work so difficult in Northern Ireland. Still, in a situation in which school education and religious education in it are mainly denominationally separate, Richardson expresses the hope that the media can help to promote a religious literacy that includes mutual understanding between Protestants and Catholics.

Section 2 (Theological, Ethical and Educational Perspectives) begins with *Jonathan Magonet's* hermeneutical and systematic *Jewish perspective* on *The Ban on Images in a Media Culture Context.* Professor Magonet, who is a rabbi and the former director of the Leo Baeck Colleges of Jewish Studies, London, makes it clear that not only the ban on images in the Hebrew Bible, but even more its prophetic tradition and the Ten Commandments offer orientation points highly relevant to present media ethics. In particular, the Ninth Commandment, "You shall not bear false witness against your neighbor", that criticizes the "tale-bearing" and "gossip" that are "the bread and butter of the media". It is Magonet's conviction that the Jewish tradition can contribute to entertaining a "healthy skepticism about the ideas and opinions" that are presented daily in the media.

Saeid Edalatnejad, Assistant Professor at the Encyclopaedia Islamica Foundation in Tehran, Iran, introduces an *Islamic perspective* on *Pictures, Symbols and the Media.* He traces the history of the prohibition of producing and using representational arts containing living creatures in the Shiite tradition. He points out that the original primary reason for this prohibition was to avoid idolatry of other gods – which is no longer a great danger in present society. Consequently, recent Islamic religious ruling has been more liberal, allowing artists and film producers a certain degree of freedom. However, there are still restrictions that hamper the artistic development especially in cinematic art.

From a *Christian, Protestant perspective Johanna Haberer*, Professor of Christian journalism, reflects on *Media Ethics as Part of a Public Theology.* Starting with the hypothesis that Christianity is a "media religion" she argues for the richness of the Christian tradition and its experiences with media in a wide sense of the word. Based on this experience, Christian theology can make substantial contributions to present ethical issues around media culture. One key concept that Haberer uses to disclose characteristics of media as well as religion is that of "attention" or "attentiveness". Christian media ethics helps to focus on the important questions of who gets how much attention in our media culture, how ethical criteria for attention management can be developed and how neglected and socially deprived people can get more attention.

As professor of educational science and media education expert, *Horst Niesyto* focuses on *Intercultural Education and the Media.* He shows that for the two presently dominant approaches of intercultural learning, the pedagogy of encounter and the conflict-oriented intercultural education, communication processes through media play an important role. Research findings on media and migration point to the challenges and chances that the media imply for the identity formation and intercultural communication of young migrants. These findings reveal that in particular music and film in popular culture offer additional modes of expression for those young people who find it difficult to communicate in written language. This is one reason why media education inside and outside schools should be promoted with an emphasis on empowering young people to express themselves, communicate competently and critically evaluate their everyday media worlds.

From a *religious education perspective, Manfred L. Pirner* argues that *Media Culture and Interreligious Learning* are more closely intertwined than is usually presumed. He starts by conceptualizing interreligious learning on the basis of conceiving the main task of education as promoting the ability to *change perspectives*: different religions and world views offer specific perspectives on the world; religious education helps to become aware of one's own perspective as one among others and to reflect on it from an observer's perspective. It is precisely this change of perspectives, Pirner argues, that is also characteristic of media reception and media use. Media education and (inter)religious education thus overlap in their subject as well as in their objectives and should therefore go hand in hand.

In their text *Religion in Journalism*, the journalists and academics *Daniel Meier* and *Peter Philipp* advance a proposal for quality and ethical standards for how journalism can and should deal with religious topics. Together with them we hope that this proposal will promote the discussion of this topic among journalists, in newspapers, radio and television.

The second proposal, presented by *Johannes Lähnemann*, offers standards for *interreligious textbook research and development*. This text has been widely discussed already by a number of outstanding international experts on interreligious dialogue and school textbook research in the context of the Nuremberg Forum. Lähnemann points out the high significance of school textbooks in shaping the students' idea of religion as well as the teachers'. The academically well-argued standards can serve as concrete guidelines for textbook development and publishing and deserve wide dissemination.

Finally, we would like to express our sincere thanks to all the contributors to this volume. Thanks also go to Martin Prowse for his help with the translation of a number of original German texts, to the University of Erlangen-Nürnberg for their financial support of the translation and to the Peter Lang publishers for adopting the book into their programme. We hope that it will stimulate further discussion, research and good practice around this important topic.

SECTON 1:
Analyses

Interrelated human rights:
freedom of religion and freedom of expression

Heiner Bielefeldt

1. Preamble: a German debate

For anyone who optimistically assumed that Germany was well on the way to a relaxed acceptance of religious pluralism based on freedom of religion and belief, rights of minorities and rights of opportunity, the public debate that started in autumn 2010 will have come as a cold shower. Thilo Sarrazin's book, "Deutschland schafft sich ab" (Germany is abolishing itself), a bleak, crisis scenario, sold more than a million copies within the first few months thus becoming a bestseller of the year (cf. Sarrazin 2010). Sarrazin simply puts the blame for various problems of integration policy – from youth crime, to failed urban development, to problems of schooling and education – on a supposedly anti-integration mentality of Islam. The controversy the book caused revealed just how much anti-Muslim resentments exist within society. Had there been a German Geert Wilders, these resentments might well have mobilised successful party political activism.

There were also surprising reactions to German President Christian Wulff's speech on the Day of German Unity 2010. His statement that Islam has become a part of Germany not only encountered unexpectedly strong objections, but also triggered a flurry of conservative efforts at "damage control". Time and again it has been said that, even though several million Muslims are now long term-residents and citizens in Germany, the country cannot be expected to take on board the cultural influence and values of Islam. Rather, Muslims who have made their home in Germany should prove their willingness to integrate by accepting the primacy of a "Judaeo-Christian culture" as the basis of national co-existence.[1] Much shriller voices on Islam or Muslims were heard in the course of public discussion and debate.[2]

---

1   It is common for the expression "Judaeo-Christian" to be used to describe the character of the German cultural landscape – or even "Leitkultur" (leading culture) – terms which are usually not only historico-descriptive, but typically also programmatic-normative. It is not, of course, intrinsically discriminating to identify a dominant historico-cultural heritage in our society, though in purely descriptive terms hyphenating Judaeo and Christian is not really sustainable, because it glosses over the discrimination of the Jews in European history. Then again, in pro-

There is another reason why the recent public debate has been both revealing and puzzling, because the broad approval Sarrazin received in surveys, blogs and message boards was not simply for what he said, but perhaps even more for his gesture of political incorrectness. To the familiar strains of: "You're surely still allowed to say ... in this country", he proclaimed his theses as the breaking of political taboos and in doing so clearly struck a chord. The fact that members of the political establishment, right up to German Chancellor Merkel, unequivocally dismissed his posturing was taken as evidence that "incorrect truths" could not be expressed openly in Germany. Talk of gagging, symbolic executions and covert censorship in the name of a supposed tyranny of political correctness appeared in letters to the editor and news comments, and was characterised by Norbert Bolz as the "Gesinnungsterror" (terror against other convictions) of the new Jacobins (cf. Bolz 2010, pp. 64–66). By contrast, Sarrazin was hailed as an enlightened and courageous person, proving, not least by using deliberately unpleasant language about minorities, that he would not be silenced.

Both with his oversimplification in his criticism of Islam and his posture of resistance against the supposed dominance of "political correctness of the elite" Sarrazin presented hinelf as an ally of Geert Wilders and other right-wing populists who believe they are defending the right to freedom of speech in Europe. Playing on anti-minority resentment is often made out to be the acid test for social non-conformity alongside resentment against anonymous political, media and cultural elites, whose alleged control and regulation of language is opposed by an aggressive, populist movement for plain speaking. Unfortunately, the political effectiveness of this approach has been demonstrated at the ballot box in several of Germany's neighbours: Austria, Denmark, the Netherlands, Switzerland and, recently, Sweden.

If we look at the recent debate on a more abstract level, we might gain the impression that some human rights norms are essentially in conflict: It may seem that we are confronted with an insurmountable antagonism of freedom of religion and belief, minority rights and anti-discrimination policies on the one hand, and free speech, including the freedom to use provocative language, on the other hand. Such an antagonistic assessment is not uncommon; it suggests that one has to decide one way or the other, or at least find some sort of a middle way.

---

grammatic-normative terms it is too narrow a construction to place on the political order of a constitutive Judaeo-Christian heritage, because it specifically excludes people not belonging to biblical tradition. For a general view on the ambivalence of the Leitkultur concept see Heiner Bielefeldt, Menschenrechte in der Einwanderungsgesellschaft. Plädoyer für einen aufgeklärten Multikulturalismus, Bielefeld 2007, pp.71 passim.

2   This is especially true of blogs and internet forums critical of Islam such as the website "Politically Incorrect ". Cf. http://www.politicallyincorrect.de.

In this article I intend to raise a fundamental objection to such a point of view. Without denying that tensions may exist between various human rights interests, my purpose is to demonstrate that the various human rights norms themselves are complementary in the sense that they mutually presuppose and mutually reinforce each other. In concrete terms: whoever wants to support freedom of religion and belief, minority rights and anti-discrimination policies must also, to be credible, be committed to freedom of expression and opinion, and in general to a climate of open discussion. The same is true the other way around in that freedom of expression cannot be defended in a credible way without taking seriously the right to freedom of thought, conscience, religion or belief. It is alarming that freedom of expression in Western Europe today is becoming more and more hijacked by right-wing populist movements. – Beginning with some basic thoughts (in section 2) on the relationship between freedom of religion and freedom of expression,[3] I will return (in section 3) to the recent debate in Germany in order to draw some practical conclusions.

2. On the "indivisibility" of freedom of religion and freedom of expression

Let me start with some general observations on the relationship between freedom of religion and freedom of expression. The final text of the World Conference on Human Rights of 1993 affirms the connection between all human rights to be "indivisible".[4] The three adjectives used at this point, "indivisible, interdependent, interrelated" are intended to make it clear that universal human rights are each premised on the others, in that each of them reinforces the others, and that the only way to make them effective is to implement them *in their entirety*. This wording from the Vienna conference on the indivisibility of human rights has since been repeated with additional emphasis in numerous UN documents.

---

3   In order not to complicate matters too much, I am limiting myself in what follows to the relationship between these two human rights. It is true that a comprehensive assessment of recent debate in Germany would have to include other human rights norms, in particular the prohibition of racial discrimination. Many prejudices against Muslims should more properly be classified as racist in that they attribute a *collective negative mentality* to certain people irrespective of their own personal religious conviction or actual religious practice, and are blind to them as individuals. Despite many areas of overlap, religious and racial discrimination should be kept conceptually quite separate given that a constitutive factor in freedom of religion as a human right is the freedom to choose for or against espousing a particular religion or world view.

4   See, World Conference on Human Rights (1993). Vienna Declaration and Programme of Action, no. 5, first sentence: "All human rights are universal, indivisible and interdependent and interrelated."

The indivisibility of all human rights more specifically also applies to the relationship between freedom of religion and freedom of expression; it is, in fact, particularly apt, for these two rights safeguard, above all, a person's *spiritual and communicative freedom* in all its dimensions, and are therefore especially close to each other.

Freedom of religion – or more properly, freedom of thought, conscience, religion or belief which also includes non-religious world views – concerns the right to independent development of the fundamental beliefs by which to live one's life. People should be free to ask elemental questions about the meaning of life, seek answers, criticise established religious or philosophical concepts, freely communicate what has been learned, lead their lives – individually or in association with others – in accordance with their religious or philosophical beliefs and pass on these beliefs and ways of life to the next generation. It is, incidentally, part of this human right, that a person may remain indifferent to such questions, show no interest in religions or philosophies, take no part in a religious community or choose not to disclose any personal beliefs.[5]

Freedom of religion (to use the short formula) is relevant to human rights as a whole because at its heart is *the dignity of the human being as agent responsible for his own actions* – the cornerstone of the human rights idea. Respect for human dignity not only comes at the beginning of the Constitution of the Federal Republic of Germany of 23 May 1949, but also of the United Nations Universal Declaration of Human Rights of 10 December 1948,[6] and would be unthinkable without respect for freedom of thought, conscience and religion.

Freedom of opinion and expression are of similar fundamental importance for human rights generally. It was Kant who described "the freedom of the pen" as "the sole palladium of the people's rights".[7] Historically freedom of opinion and expression belongs predominantly to political debate, which can only be productive if people feel free to form their own opinions, take information from different sources and impart opinions thus formed openly and without fear of repression; this applies particularly when a view deviates from the mainstream of society or politics. Freedom of expression requires, therefore, to be broadly inter-

---

5 Freedom of religion is both positive and negative – two sides of the same coin – and neither aspect should be played off against the other.

6 The preamble to the UN Declaration begins with the "recognition of the inherent dignity and of the equal and inalienable rights of all members of the human family". For the connection between human dignity and human rights see Heiner Bielefeldt (2012), Freedom of religion or belief – a human right under pressure, in Oxford Journal of Law and Religion, Vol. 1, pp. 1–21.

7 Immanuel Kant, Über den Gemeinspruch "Das mag in der Theorie richtig sein, taugt aber nicht für die Praxis" (On the common saying, "That may be right in theory, but it won't work in practice"), in: Kant Werke. Akademie-Ausgabe, vol. VIII, p. 304.

preted and can include information or ideas which, in the frequently-cited formulation of the European Court of Human Rights, may "offend, shock or disturb the State or any sector of the population" (ECHR, 07.12.1976, Handyside, Ser. A/24, para. no. 49.)

As with freedom of religion or belief, freedom of opinion and expression is also about the right to a *spiritual and communicative freedom*, and here the connection with public discourse, is even more marked (cf. Schwartländer 1986). Its importance for human rights in general lies precisely in its function of enabling public expression. Indeed, whether human rights can be implemented fully rests crucially on whether there is a culture of critical public debate in which people are active in defending fundamental rights – their own as well as other people's – and openly address failings, infringements and denials. That is why the German Federal Constitutional Court set out, in a much cited opinion in 1958, that freedom of expression is "in a certain sense the basis of *every* freedom whatsoever".[8] This statement is to be understood literally. Without freedom of expression there would be, strictly speaking, neither freedom of association, freedom to join a trades union, freedom to found a political party, nor effective guarantees of free elections or fair judicial procedures, and without it there would also be no human right to freedom of religion or belief.

The intrinsic affinity of freedom of religion and freedom of expression – including the understanding that the one *is premised on the other*, meaning that both must be realised *together* – does not deny possible tensions. In extreme cases aggressively polemical or inflammatory statements about minorities may create a climate in which members of these minorities are too afraid to profess their faith, that is, to exercise their right to freedom of religion without fear. The "indivisibility" of human rights does not presuppose a harmonious relationship, nor an easy win-win-situation. Indeed, situations can occur in which striking a balance and seeking compromise may be unavoidable, and, guided by the postulate of indivisibility, one then will have to attempt to *do justice* – as far as possible – to *all the human rights issues under debate*. Strict criteria are applied to any such balancing exercise and to any human rights restrictions that may follow, and are intended to safeguard the essence of the human rights, even in cases of conflict.[9]

---

8   "Es ist in gewissem Sinne die Grundlage *jeder* Freiheit überhaupt" (Italics in original), BVerfGE, vol. 7, p. 198.

9   For the problem of restrictions see Kälin, Walter / Künzli, Jörg (2005), Universeller Menschenrechtsschutz, Basel/ Baden-Baden: Helbing Lichtenhahn, pp. 104ff. The International Covenant on Civil and Political Rights (1966) guarantees the freedom of expression (Article 19) and follows with the obligation on states to prohibit by law "any advocacy of racial or religious hatred"

The danger for the way human rights are perceived and realised is if the experience of *concrete* conflict is construed as an *abstract antagonism*; if the indivisibility of human rights – that is, the one premised on the others – threatens to fall by the wayside. As far as the relationship between freedom of religion and freedom of expression is concerned, this danger undoubtedly exists. There has been a tendency in recent years in international discussion on human rights for freedom of religion and freedom of expression to be deliberately set *against each other*, which always ends up damaging understanding and the chances of realising both these two rights.

For instance, in the context of freedom of religion or belief it is sometimes falsely supposed that this right stands in an inherent opposition to freedom of expression. The assumption is that freedom of religion or belief, inter alia, has the function of putting a limit to an "overly extensive" use of freedom of expression. The best known recent example of this tendency is the fight against what has been termed "defamation of religions". Over more than a decade the Organisation of Islamic Cooperation (OIC), an intergovernmental body currently composed of 57 member States,[10] regularly tabled resolutions in the UN Commission on Human Rights, General Assembly and Human Rights Council on the issue of "combating defamation of religions". Although these resolutions typically triggered fierce debates, they finally always received a majority of votes.[11] The controversy peaked during the notorious Danish cartoon crisis in 2006 which had triggered an outcry in large parts of the Muslim world. Although it is understandable that many Muslims feel offended by those polemical cartoons, political calls for combating such and other "defamations" can easily pave the way for authoritarian policies of censorship, criminalization and other restrictive measures which would collide with freedom of expression – and freedom of religion or belief, too (Cf. Temperman 2008, pp. 485–516). Indeed, the main problem of the OIC resolutions on defamation is that they appear to legitimize draconian measures, such as anti-blasphemy laws, which typically have intimidating effects on members of religious minorities as well as on critics or dissenters. In Pa-

---

(Article 20). But the threshold for such restrictions must be kept high to avoid harming the culture of public expression of opinion.

10 The OIC's previous name "Organisation of the Islamic Conference" was changed in June 2011 to "Organisation of Islamic Cooperation".

11 Cf. Commission on Human Rights resolutions 1999/82, 2000/84, 2001/4, 2002/9, 2003/4, 2004/6 and 2005/3; General Assembly resolutions 60/150, 61/164, 62/154, 63/171, 64/156 and 65/224; Human Rights Council resolutions 4/9, 7/19, 10/22 and 13/16. For a critical assessment cf. Blitt, Robert C. (2011), The Bottom Up Journey of "Defamation of Religions" from Muslim States to the United Nations: A Case Study of the Migration of Anti-Constitutional Ideas, in: Studies in Law, Politics and Society, Vol. 56, pp. 121–211.

kistan, one of the leading countries within the OIC and an initiator of various defamation resolutions, ill-defined blasphemy offences can even lead to a death sentence (cf. Freedom House 2010, pp. 69–87).

Another problem is that the OIC resolutions convey the impression that *religions per se* – and in particular Islam – should somehow be entitled to international legal protection of their reputation. It remains unclear who in practice could claim such a protection: religious authorities, the majority of believers, or States pretending to operate in the service of (one or more) religions? Be that as it may, the idea of protecting the honour of religions is clearly at variance with the human rights approach which institutionalizes due respect for the dignity and freedom of *human beings* rather than protecting religions as such. It would thus be a grave misunderstanding to somehow associate freedom of religion or belief with the fight against defamation of religions. In the end, this would even amount to turning the human right to freedom of religion or belief upside down.

After more than a decade of bitter controversies in different UN forums around this issue, no resolution on defamation of religions was tabled in 2011. Instead, the OIC submitted to the UN Human Rights Council a resolution on "Combating intolerance, negative stereotyping and stigmatization of, and discrimination, incitement to violence and violence against persons based on religion or belief". This Human Rights Council resolution 16/18 was adopted without a vote on 24 March 2011, and the UN General Assembly adopted a resolution with the same title on 19 December 2011.[12] As the somewhat complicated title shows, the purpose is protection of human beings rather than safeguarding the reputation of religions. Whether Human Rights Council resolution 16/18 actually marks a turning point in the international debate, however, remains to be seen in the future. What one can say for the time being is that it harbours new opportunities to address in a more open inter-group atmosphere important political issues, like stereotypes, prejudices and concomitant manifestations of extreme hatred. This certainly is a positive development. It would be naïve, however, to assume that the controversial issues previously discussed under the heading of defamation of religions have now definitely been settled.

Western Governments mostly voted against the OIC resolutions on defamation, and they had good reasons for doing so. On closer investigation, however, things look less clear also in the West (Cf. Nash 2007). For instance, some European States continue to have domestic anti-blasphemy provisions in their criminal law books (Cf. European Commission for Democracy through Law (Venice Commission) 2008). Even the wording of some of the historical judgments of the

---

12   Cf. Human Rights Council resolution 16/18 of 24 March 2011 and UN General Assembly resolution 66/167 of 19 December 2011.

European Court of Human Rights remained ambiguous in that they could convey the impression that religious feelings should be protected against offensive expressions deemed "blasphemous" by some believers.[13] It is thus useful to recall what Asma Jahangir, then UN Special Rapporteur on freedom of religion or belief, pointed out at the peak of the Danish cartoon crisis, i.e. that there is no right to be free from criticism or even ridicule.[14] Establishing such a right would indeed destroy the very preconditions of an open and pluralistic society based on equal respect for everyone's dignity and freedom.

Indeed, a supposedly "essentially" antagonistic construction which sets freedom of religion generally against freedom of expression is not only damaging to freedom of expression; it also obscures the human rights content of freedom of religion itself, and in extreme cases can even turn into the exact opposite. It is a mistaken belief that freedom of religion entails a right to protection of religious feelings, religious identity or a de facto dominance of a certain religion by restricting freedom of expression, and threatens to lose sight, at least in part, of the freedom-related core of religious freedom (See Freedom House 2010). In such a situation, it is hardly appropriate to speak of *freedom* of religion – unless one includes the *freedom* of certain religions not to face critical questions or the presence of competing ideas, but this would mean abandoning the basic intention of the human rights.

3. Overcoming resentment and prejudice through a culture of public debate

Let us now return to the recent debate in Germany and to the political challenges it has thrown up. What conclusions can be drawn from the issues discussed, especially in relation to international conflict, to assist current debate in Germany? In matters of human rights – here freedom of religion or belief and freedom of opinion and expression – it is important in domestic debate, too, to safeguard the *indivisible connection* between them, and whenever possible to give both rights equal prominence. Two things follow from this. Firstly (and this should be a minimum condition), a commitment to freedom of religion – often linked to minority rights and equality of opportunity – should never give the impression of

---

13   Cf. ECtHR, Otto Preminger v. Austria (appl. 13470/87) of 20 September 1994.
14   Cf. Report of the Special Rapporteur on freedom of religion or belief, Asma Jahangir, and the Special Rapporteur on contemporary forms of racism, racial discrimination, xenophobia and related intolerance, Doudou Diène, further to Human Rights Council decision 1/107 on incitement to racial and religious hatred and the promotion of tolerance, A/HRC/2/3, at paragraph 36.

being at the expense of freedom of expression and a culture of open debate. Secondly, it is crucial that enthusiasm for freedom of expression should not be left to right-wing populist movements.

Let us be clear, religious freedom is not only under threat from *state* persecution or discrimination, but can also be impaired by *society's* prejudices and resentments against particular religious or ideological groups. For this reason, efforts to overcome stereotypical perceptions and resentment-laden prejudices belong in a broad sense to what freedom of religion demands of state and society.[15] The flood of anti-Muslim resentment caused by the recent Sarrazin controversy shows just how essential such efforts are. To be credible in terms of human rights these have to take place in a climate of open debate where the value placed on the right to free speech is tested in practice.

It would be misguided, for example, to say that expressing scepticism, criticism or even fear of Islam, or Muslims, is wrong or should be taboo. It is more a case of treating reservations and anxieties *sensitively* in public debate, examining them critically for partial factual accuracy, eradicating negative stereotyping and oversimplified information, confronting personal slurs decisively. In an enlightened culture of debate the dividing line is between accuracy and cliché, not between sympathetic and unsympathetic representations of Islam (cf. Bielefeld 2009). Acknowledging shades of difference is more than a purely academic exercise – it is a *fundamental principle of fairness*.[16] It is about the ability to look and to listen, to be prepared to read between the lines, not to put individuals and their views in a box or subsume them within a supposed unchangeable collective mentality.

Anti-Muslim sentiments are clearly widespread in society and cannot be dispelled through well-meaning regulations on language use. Nor would it suffice to draw up examples of "good practice" in order to improve the generally negative image of Islam under which many Muslims in Germany are suffering today (See Bundesministerium des Inneren 2007, p. 109). Superficial attempts at focusing just on good practice examples would be likely to fuel mistrust. Instead, efforts should be directed towards laying reservations openly on the table; to discuss,

---

15 In the context of human rights the primary obligation always lies with the state. In addition to its duties as a state, it has the "obligation to respect" that religious freedom limits legitimate state interference; the "obligation to protect" religious freedom against possible restrictions by third parties; and the "obligation to promote" an atmosphere of tolerance in the whole of society, conducive to attaining true freedom of religion.

16 This includes not accepting single-cause explanations, especially those with a one-sided focus on cultural or religious considerations; it also means overcoming cultural essentialist ideas which suppose Islam to be an unchanging entity, virtually blind to individuals as agents responsible for their own actions.

argue, exchange divergent opinions and assessments, break down prejudices, and ultimately achieve clearer understanding. Nietzsche was right to say that resentment blooms in hidden places (cf. Nietzsche 1976). It flourishes under cover or at least round the pub tables (the equivalent today may be anonymous websites), and this is the reason why supposed taboo-breakers like Thilo Sarrazin can stage the heroic posture of "telling it like it is" where others only have unformed thoughts, or speak behind their hands. If, however, the issues he espouses are debated openly and robustly, then the dramatic breaking of taboos loses its impact.

Overcoming stereotypical perceptions about minorities necessarily implies being critical of the media, but this should not descend into a wholesale attack on the media. Criticism of the media can only achieve change if it is accompanied by a general acknowledgment of the important role journalists play in a democratic culture of dialogue,[17] and an appreciation of the often arduous conditions under which media professionals work. It is true that journalists in our part of the world do not expect to be physically assaulted, or risk life, freedom and health.[18] Nevertheless, it is worrying enough that, as a professional group, they are generally held in low esteem in society and often work in conditions of extreme competitive stress and uncertain social standing. Apart from focusing on negative stereotpying, inaccuracies and misleading exaggeration, criticism of the media should look to improve the structural conditions for fairness, diversity and quality. A question might be, what action is needed to counter hasty journalistic decisions, superficial personalisation and dramatic polarisation? How could the media become more accessible to the active involvement of minorities, including religious minorities? Should the right of reply be given stronger legal protection, and if so, what guarantee could be given that it would not result in negative consequences for freedom of the media? How can schools identify and act upon opportunities for media education and media literacy?[19]

Furthermore, it is timely to recall that the meaning of freedom of expression and opinion is, in the words of the German Federal Constitutional Court "in a

---

17 In the course of their work journalists need to be assured that, for example, they will not be put under surveillance, that they have the right to refuse to give information in order to protect their sources. Such rights are not "privileges", but essential conditions to ensure that public debate can take place in the media.

18 It is clear from reports received from the NGO "Reporter ohne Grenzen" (Reporters without Borders) and from documentation of the UN Special Rapporteurs on the right to freedom of opinion and expression or on the situation of human rights defenders, that journalists, publishers and other media professionals are exposed to threats in many places. Many states make use of censorship and intimidation – often in very sophisticated ways – employing not only the police and security services, but also departments of finance and trade.

19 For more on these and other issues see also, Article 19. Global Campaign For Free Expression (ed.), The Camden Principles on Freedom of Expression and Equality (April 2009).

certain sense the basis of *every* freedom". A general dissatisfaction with the ubiquitousness of the media and the cheap attacks to which they sadly often lend themselves may partly explain why belief in the importance of journalistic freedom of expression – as representative of the universal freedom of expression – is being eroded. At all events, it would be disastrous if the emphasis on freedom of speech in Western Europe today were thought to reside in the right-wing populist movements who stage themselves as heroes in the fight against a supposed tyranny of political correctness and pad out their own subversive incorrectness with vile comments against Muslims and other minorities. It is aggravating and, more than that, a cause for alarm that someone like Geert Wilders, who is so anti-dialogue and runs his party strictly as a one-man enterprise, should be able, with some success in public, to call himself the defender of freedom of speech in Europe. There is reason to fear that his posturing will be gratefully seized upon by extremists in some parts of the Islamic world as confirmation that freedom of expression in the West has degenerated into being an instrument of propaganda against Islam, and that the media should be held on a much tighter rein.

In rejecting, as we must, prejudice against Muslims and all sorts of right-wing populist tendencies, it would be a huge political mistake to contemplate applying any restrictive measures to freedom of expression or freedom of the media, as this would only be grist for the mill of extremists. The exact opposite is needed: not less freedom of expression, but more freedom of expression, more pluralism in the media, more argument and debate, more fairness, more imaginative and creative criticism and counter-criticism. Only in this way can resentment against minorities in society be overcome in the long term. And at the same time, the claim by Sarrazin and Co. to be tellers of "uncomfortable truths" will be exposed as empty posturing.

The best and most efficient way of countering hate speech is in fact *alternative speech*: public statements of solidarity, fair media reporting and clarifications aimed at eliminating negative stereotypes. A main result of a number of regional workshops organized by the Office of the High Commissioner for Human Rights in 2011 on "incitement to hatred" was that, in order to cope with hate speech, we need *more speech* in the sense of public initiatives, well-qualified media work and enhanced inter-group communication.[20] Among other things, this always presupposes freedom of expression. Thus, even in a situation where some acts of "free speech" actually threaten the rights of religious minorities, it would be wrong to assume a general antagonism between freedom of religion

---

20   Cf. the joint submissions by three Special Rapporteurs to the 2011 OHCHR expert workshops on the prohibition of incitement to national, racial or religious hatred, available online at: http://www.ohchr.org/EN/Issues/FreedomOpinion/Articles19-20/Pages/Index.aspx.

and freedom of expression. The opposite is true: We can have freedom of religion only by working on behalf of more freedom of expression, a human right way too precious to leave it to populist movements.

References

Bielefeldt, Heiner (2009), *Das Islambild in Deutschland. Zum öffentlichen Umgang mit der Angst vor dem Islam.* 2nd enlarged ed., Berlin: Deutsches Institut für Menschenrechte.

Bielefeldt, Heiner (2012), Freedom of religion or belief – a human right under pressure, in: *Oxford Journal of Law and Religion* 1, pp. 1–21.

Bolz, Norbert (2010), Die neuen Jakobiner, in: *FOCUS,* No. 37/10, 13 September 2010, pp. 64–66.

Bundesministerium des Inneren (2007), *Muslime in Deutschland. Integration, Integrationsbarrieren, Religion und Einstellungen zu Demokratie, Rechtsstaat und politisch-religiös motivierter Gewalt,* edited by Karin Brettfeld and Peter Wetzels, Bonn: BMI, Referat P II 1; Rostock: Publ.-Versand der Bundesregierung.

ECHR, 07.12.1976, Handyside, Ser. A/24, para. no. 49.

European Commission for Democracy through Law (Venice Commission) (2008), *Report on the relationship between freedom of religion and freedom of religion: The issue of regulation and prosecution of blasphemy, religious insult and incitement to religious hatred, Council of Europe Doc. CDL-AD(2008)026.*

Freedom House (2010), *Policing Belief: The Impact on Blasphemy Laws on Human Rights,* Washington: Freedom House.

Kant, Immanuel (1900ff.), *Werke.* Akademie-Ausgabe, vol. VIII.

Nash, David (2007), *Blasphemy in the Christian World. A History,* Oxford: OUP.

Nietzsche, Friedrich (1976), *Zur Genealogie der Moral,* Stuttgart: Kröner.

Sarrazin, Thilo (2010), *Deutschland schafft sich ab. Wie wir unser Land aufs Spiel setzen,* München: audio media verlag.

Schwartländer, Johannes / Willoweit, Dietmar (eds.) (1986), *Meinungsfreiheit – Grundgedanken und Entwicklung in Europa und USA,* Kehl: Norbert Paul Engel Verlag.

Temperman, Jeroen (2008), Blasphemy, Defamation of Religions and Human Rights Law, in: *Netherlands Quaterly of Human Rights* 26, No.4, pp. 485–516.

Media legislation in Islamic countries

Mathias Rohe

1. Introduction

It is rare to find opinions on freedom of expression argued from the perspective of Islam. For centuries, as in Europe, it was not considered relevant to religious debate. But, unlike the situation in Europe, the Islamic world has remained largely unchanged to this day. Why is this?

It must be acknowledged, first, that there are Muslims who speak out for freedom of expression. But for all the individual differences, even today in many parts of the Islamic world freedom of expression and especially freedom of belief are not in good shape. Freedom of belief is mentioned here because speaking openly in public about religion is a major issue. Events such as the murder of Egyptian Christians and Christian missionaries in Turkey, the execution of Bahá'i is in Iran, the destruction of churches in Malaysia in the row over the use of the Arabic word for God (Allah) make depressing reading. An extreme case recently concerned a Christian woman, Asia Bibi, sentenced to death by a regional court in Pakistan under the blasphemy law allegedly for having insulted Muhammad and the Qur'an (See the detailed report Kazim 2010). Shortly after, the Governor of Punjab Province, Salman Taseer, who had called for the repeal of the blasphemy law invoked in the Bibi case, was shot dead by a security guard. This law permits the death sentence for anyone insulting Islam, the Qur'an or the Prophet Muhammad.[1] Over new year 2011 tens of thousands of Islamists demonstrated against any relaxing of the law, and hundreds of clerics celebrated the murderer's action.[2] The Pope's criticism of the law as a gross violation of human rights was described bizarrely by Islamists as a pretext for plunging the whole world into a deadly war.[3]

Advocates of freedom of expression in Iran also live dangerously. For example, Hossein Derakhshan, the Iranian-Canadian blogger, was fined and sentenced to over 19 years in prison because of his on-line commentaries. He was charged

---

1   See "Gouverneur des Punjab in Islamabad erschossen", FAZ 05.01.11, p. 5.
2   See the report "Geistliche feiern Mord in Pakistan" of 05.01.11, accessed on 07.11.12 at www.n-tv.de/politik/Geistliche-feiern-Mord-in-Pakistan-article2296046.html
3   See, for example, "Pakistan weist Kritik des Papstes an Blasphemiegesetz zurück", FAZ 12.01.11, p. 4.

with "anti-government propaganda", "insulting religious sanctity" and "creating and managing vulgar and obscene websites".[4] The Iranian film director Jafar Panahi was prosecuted for "assembly and colluding with the intention to commit crimes against the national security" and "propaganda against the Islamic Republic". He was given a 6-year suspended sentence and a 20-year ban on travel and all forms of film work.[5] This ragbag of charges reveals the main thrust of state-sponsored repression: the primary concern is to defend a brutal dictatorship, religious issues being of secondary importance. The fact that there is no freedom of expression in states with majority Muslim populations can be explained primarily by the fact that generally the rule of law does not prevail; instead rule is arbitrary and manifests itself in various forms of authoritarianism. This is true of both secular regimes and those with religious orientation.

One incident – having very little to do with Islam – was published by WikiLeaks,[6] in which, during a heated exchange in the Supreme Council for National Security, the Iranian president was slapped in the face by the chief of the Revolutionary Guard for suggesting (surprisingly) more freedom of the press. Such events are not unique in the history of the Islamic world. The historically remarkable, relatively liberal attitudes towards other religions had clear limits; there was (and is) no true equality even if the scholars who took an active part in violence against religious minorities – such as the 13th century scholar Ibn Taymiyyah (cf. Krawietz, 2003, pp. 39ff., 40 with footnote. 5 ff.) – were few in number.

The brave individuals who speak out for freedom of expression in these regions usually do so in the context of global consensus around the UN Charter of Human Rights, and participate in a debate with few religious connotations or arguments. Where religious aspects of Islam are involved they usually relate to freedom of belief. The general trend is towards restriction: open discussion of religion is largely taboo; criticism of Islamic positions, especially, tends to be vigorously opposed and can result in massive discrimination and persecution of non-Muslims.

Even in mediaeval times it was common for religious disputes simply not to be pursued. Middle Eastern cultures generally prefer not to air substantive differences in the open, but rather to pass over matters of disagreement in polite silence or to find some indirect way of offering criticism. Argument conducted in language that is openly critical is often taken as a personal attack that questions

---

4   Report "19 Jahre Haft für Blogger", in Amnesty Journal 01/2011, p. 12.
5   See report "Ein leerer Stuhl klagt an", Die Zeit 30.12.10, p. 46.
6   Report in the Tagesspiegel 30.12.10 ("Wikileaks: Ahmadinedschad bei Sitzung geohrfeigt"), accessed at www.tagesspiegel.de/politik/wikileaks-ahmadinedschad-bei-sitzung-geohrfeigt/3685018.html

the individual's right to recognition and is therefore flatly rejected (cf. Kamali 1997, esp. pp. 152ff.). This is consistent with the author's own experience of several years' residence in the region. A case in point in early 2011 was the furious reaction of the Egyptian government to the Pope's carefully worded criticism of the murder of Coptic Christians and the lack of protection for minorities in Egypt.[7] However, this complete shutting down of debate is gradually giving way in many Islamic states under the influence of the new media such as the internet.

Having said this, it is still rare in many parts of the Islamic world for opinions and discussions to relate directly to freedom of expression, especially those drawing on religious argument and conviction. We should not forget that many Muslims do defend minority groups and oppose repression, without necessarily doing so for specifically religious motives.

2. Other positions

1. Introduction

As has been said, the traditional literature on religious law contains no direct examination of freedom of expression, though it is true that some signs can be found in Islamic tradition. For example, the ancient principle in Islamic law of consultation (shura) (cf. Badry 1998) does indeed imply that one may express one's opinion, but not if libellous or slanderous (cf. Kamali 1997, pp. 117ff.). Three position statements follow which, given the importance and standing of the originating body or individual, are of particular significance.

2. The Cairo Declaration on Human Rights in Islam, 1990

In 1990 the member states of the Organisation of the Islamic Conference (OIC) adopted the Cairo Declaration on Human Rights in Islam which sets out a modern opinion on the right to freedom of expression.[8] The declaration can be seen as a response to the UN Human Rights Charter which is repeatedly cited in criticism of Islamic states for infringing human rights. Its intention is to document the fact that Islam possessed a balanced, in fact divinely legitimised system of

---

7   See report "Misr tastad'i safirataha laday al-Vatikan li l-tašawwur", al-Hayat 12.01.11, p. 4. The Egyptian Foreign Minister objects strongly to the Pope's comments because, he says, they will exacerbate religious tensions.

8   English text accessed 31.10.11 at www1.umn.edu/humanrts/instree/cairodeclaration.html

human rights long before the discredited "Western import" human rights documents. The primacy of Islam and sharia permeate the whole document. A few relevant articles are cited here:

Article 10

"Islam is the religion of true unspoiled nature. It is prohibited to exercise any form of pressure on man or to exploit his poverty or ignorance in order to force him to change his religion to another religion or to atheism."

Article 19

d) *"There shall be no crime or punishment except as provided for in the Shari'ah."*

Article 22

a) *"Everyone shall have the right to express his opinion freely in such manner as would not be contrary to the principles of the Shari'ah.*
b) *Everyone shall have the right to advocate what is right, and propagate what is good, and warn against what is wrong and evil according to the norms of Islamic Shari'ah.[9]*
c) *Information is a vital necessity to society. It may not be exploited or misused in such a way as may violate sanctities and the dignity of Prophets, undermine moral and ethical values or disintegrate, corrupt or harm society or weaken its faith."*

Article 24

"All the rights and freedoms stipulated in this Declaration are subject to the Islamic Shari'ah."

From this it is clear that freedom of expression and opinion as contained in the 1948 UN Charter, and other international agreements and constitutional provisions, is addressed only in formal terms; in substantive terms it lags far behind. When, as already noted, sharia can be interpreted as sanctioning massive persecution, even death, then rights under sharia law are virtually meaningless.

---

9   This is the old principle of "amr bi l-maʿrūf wa l-nahy ʿan al-munkar"; see Rohe 2009, p. 41.

3. The Arab Charter on Human Rights 2004

The follow-up document, the Arab Charter on Human Rights 2004,[10] draws heavily on the UN Human Rights Charter and represents a substantive advance over the Cairo declaration of 1990. The relevant provisions are contained in Articles 30 and 32:

Article 30

1. *"Everyone has the right to freedom of thought, conscience and religion and no restrictions may be imposed on the exercise of such freedom except as provided for by law."*

Article 32

1. *"The present Charter guarantees the right to information and to freedom of opinion and expression, as well as the right to seek, receive and impart information and ideas through any medium, regardless of geographical boundaries.*
2. *Such rights and freedoms shall be exercised in conformity with the fundamental values of society and shall be subject only to such limitations as are required to ensure respect for the rights of reputation of others or the protection of national security, public order and public health or morals."*

Nevertheless, despite previous criticism of the Cairo declaration, the Arab Charter on Human Rights refers in its preamble and in certain articles (such as Article 3) to sharia,[11] thereby undermining its potential compatibility with the UN Charter. In this respect it raises the same objections as the Cairo declaration. What is more, there are no effective implementation mechanisms or even reporting structures.

---

10 It was ratified by seven countries and came into force on 15.03.2008; it has since been implemented in 10 Arab states; for the content see. e.g. Wittinger 2008, pp. 63ff. The English text can be found at www1.umn.edu/humanrts/instree/loas2005.html?msource=UNWDEC19001&tr=y&auid=3337655.
11 "Sharia" is a highly flexible and multifaceted system of norms and interpretation in Islam. From a human rights perspective, the interpretations still dominant today which allow the unequal treatment of the sexes, religions and world views, are problematic. For greater detail see Rohe 2010, pp.141ff.

4. The work of Mohammed Hashim Kamali

One of the few writers on freedom of expression in Islam is Mohammed Hashim Kamali. Born in Afghanistan and now teaching law and jurisprudence in Malaysia, Kamali is a highly respected and dedicated scholar of international reputation.[12] Deploying classical reasoning, but from a modern perspective, Kamali derives freedom of expression from the two principal sources of Islam, the Qur'an and the Sunnah (Prophetic traditions). A starting point for Kamali is Sura 4, 148 in the Qur'an: "God does not like evil to be uttered in public except by him who has been wronged" (English translation from Bobzin 2010). Kamali understands this to mean that bad, obscene, immoral or other harmful language is strictly forbidden, but not when justice demands it, if, for example, it gives the oppressed a voice. Justice, he argues, is inseparable from right and truth, and may, in a case of conflict, outweigh the personal dignity of the individual (Op. cit., p.9.). Freedom of expression is complementary to the Qur'anic [13] dignity of the individual who should have the right to express opinions and ideas which concern him (Op. cit., p.11.). Kamali also cites the normative sharia principle of "ibāha aslīya": what is not explicitly forbidden is permissible (Op. cit., p.15).

In a number of Islamic doctrines established as normative Kamali finds firm evidence for freedom of speech and opinion: for example, the Qur'anic doctrine of "hisbah" (enjoin what is good, prohibit what is evil) for him includes freedom of opinion, because without the latter effective implementation of the former would be impossible (Op. cit., pp. 28ff.). The same is true of the Qur'anic concept of good counsel ("nasīha"), part of the injunction to promote what is good and prevent what is evil (Op. cit., pp. 34ff.). Kamali also mentions the key Islamic-political doctrine of "shura" (counsel) enshrined in the Qur'an as being crucial to freedom of expression (Op. cit., pp. 40ff.). For the interpretation of Islamic norms he refers to the fundamental principle of independent reasoning ("ijtihâd") (Op. cit., pp. 45ff) as well as the historically documented freedom to offer criticism (of rulers) (Op. cit., pp. 49ff.).

In a later section Kamali examines freedom of opinion ("hurrīyat al-ra'y") in more detail (Op. cit., pp. 61ff.) and he finds a basis for this in the history of Islamic norms: the concept of individual opinion ("ra'y") originally had a positive

---

12   The text used here is Kamali 1994.
13   Kamali cites Sure 17, 70: And indeed We have honoured the Children of Adam, and We have carried them on land and sea, and have provided them with At-Taiyibāt (lawful good things), and have preferred them above many of those whom We have created with a marked preference.

connotation. The often quoted basis for it, even if of doubtful authenticity,[14] was a conversation between Muhammad and a man who later became an administrator and judge.[15] Before appointing Mu'ādh ibn Jabal as a judge[16] in the Yemen, Muhammad is said to have asked him how he would pass judgements. Mu'ādh replied that he would first refer to God's Word; then, if necessary, to the Sunnah of the Prophet. Thereafter he would endeavour tirelessly to make his own judgement ("ajtahidu bi ra'yī").[17] This key concept in verbal form denotes the flexibility and contiuning development of Islamic law: ijtihâd (derived from the Arabic verb ajtahidu), independent, rational common sense.

Given the many unresolved legal issues in the Qur'an and in the early formulation of the hadiths the rational approach must have been the general rule. It was not by chance that the representatives of the law schools were known as the "ahl al-ra'y" (the people of legal opinion). Goldziher (1884, pp. 18ff.) writes that originally "fiqh" (teaching of standards) and "ra'y" were semantically equivalent. There is evidence (cf. Ibn Khaldūn 1986, p. 446; Motzki 1991, pp. 17 ff..; Hallaq 2005, pp. 74ff.; Melchert 1997, pp. 1ff.) from the 8th century A.D. of disagreement between the "ahl al-ra'y" and "the ahl al-hadīṯ" people of the hadith). The latter preferred a closer association with the Prophetic tradition, even though the sharp distinction drawn later between the two schools was not a true reflection of the situation. Clearly the concept of "ra'y" underwent a change in meaning with increasingly negative connotations. If the authenticity of the conversation between Muhammad and Mu'ādh ibn Jabal is accepted, then "ra'y" has a positive connotation, and was only later considered to be arbitrary and an infringement of norms. Kamali argues that "ra'y" should not be understood in this way, but that its foundations and objectives are not only desirable, but essential.

Kamali also addresses the specific fact relevant to both freedom of opinion and freedom of belief that it is prohibited to insult the Prophet (Muhammad) ("sabb al-nabī") (Op. cit., pp. 212 ff.). Considered a form of apostasy, it also carries the death sentence, with many scholars rejecting repentance as grounds for waiving punishment (cf. Peters 2005, p. 65; wizārat al-auqāf wa l-šu'ūn al-Isālmīya, al-Kuwait, al-mausū'a al-fiqhīya, pp. 184ff.), and can be taken as justi-

---

14 However, there is the statement in Muhammad's "sermon of farewell" (khutbat al-wadāʿ) in Ibn Hišām 1975, p. 186) that one ought not to depart from the Holy Book and the "sunnah" of his Prophet.

15 Its authenticity is nevertheless disputed; for different opinions see Lucas 2006, pp. 289, 317ff.; Jokisch 2007, pp. 526ff.

16 The sources for his areas of responsibility are contradictory: some state that he was sent as governor following a military campaign or as a teacher of the Qur'an; see Tyan 1960, pp. 70 ff.

17 Recorded, e.g. in musnad des Ahmad ibn Hanbal vol. 5 (edition Beirut 1413/1993), pp. 272ff. (no. 22068); cited e.g. in Salqīnī 1991, pp. 73, 142; for critique see Muslehuddin 1975, p. 44.

fication for the persecution of people of other faiths as in the case of modern Pakistan or the violent protests at the publication of the Muhammad cartoons. There was the altogether bizarre case of death threats against an English teacher in Sudan whose class had voted to name a teddy bear "Muhammad",[18] and similar threats against a Pakistani businessman who threw away the business card of someone named Muhammad.[19]

Kamali sets out in detail why apostasy and blasphemy are different in sharia law; he also argues against the severe sanctions of sharia for blasphemy. Although he does not altogether oppose it being a (mild) punishable offence, he makes it clear that it is the connection with matters of state security rather than the religious aspects that justifies the punishment (Op. cit., pp. 214ff, 242ff.).

Repressive laws typical of dictatorships in many Islamic countries are generally accompanied by severe restrictions on freedom of expression. As far as religious expression is concerned, Islamic political interests impose massive restrictions which not only inhibit debate within Islam, but hugely restrict non-Muslims in what they can say and do. The very broad definition of prohibition[20] often goes hand in hand with arbitrary justice. Even the formal declarations of human rights of 1990 and 2004 contain significant opportunities for imposing restrictions and a considerable degree of legal uncertainty. Furthermore, the use of the same terminology does not always lead to the same outcome. It has long been realised from attempts to harmonise laws in different parts of the world that the preconceptions and social environment of those interpreting the law can significantly affect the interpretation of norms. In the absence of institutions such as the European Court of Justice or the European Court of Human Rights there are certain to be widely differing outcomes. This is even more true for such abstract legal concepts as freedom of expression which leave much room for interpretation.

---

18 See report "Sudanesen fordern den Tod der britischen Lehrerin" 30.11.07, accessed 07.11.12 at www.welt.de/vermischtes/article1416957/Sudanesen_fordern_Tod_der_britischen_Lehrerin. html

19 See report "Blasphemie in Arztpraxis" 13.12.10, accessed 07.11.12 at http://archiv.sueddeutsche.de/f5538B/3780098/Blasphemie-in-Arztpraxis.html

20 See e.g. the current ruling of the Muslim Law Enactment, §172 in Selangor and the Federal Territory of Kuala Lumpur in Malaysia: "Whoever by words spoken or written or by visible representations insults or brings into contempt or attempts to insult or bring into contempt the Muslim religion or the tenets of any sect thereof or the teaching of any lawfully authorized religious teacher or any fatwa (religious edict) lawfully issued by the President (of the State Religious Council) or under the provisions of this Enactment shall be punishable with imprisonment for a term not exceeding six months or with a fine not exceeding one thousand dollars" (cited in Kamali 1997, p. 286).

3. Outlook

Religious debate within Islam on the extent and limitations of freedom of expression is still in its infancy, and is overlaid with political and cultural considerations. The largely hostile reactions to the Muhammad cartoons first published in Denmark in 2005 may therefore stem from a general cultural and communicative understanding which does its best to avoid disputes on religious matters.

In countries such as Saudi Arabia or Iran, Islam is invoked to legitimise the regimes and their prevailing interpretation which is extremely restrictive of any kind of freedom of expression. But even where political power derives primarily from other principles of legitimacy, the effect of the majority form of Islam as found in many parts of the Islamic world is a considerable restriction on freedom of opinion and belief because in all matters of the law and society Islam takes precedence.[21] Conversion to Islam, for example, is encouraged, whereas conversion from Islam is obstructed, and in some states carries the death penalty, and recruitment to other religions is simply forbidden.

Issues which are hotly debated at present are the extent of restrictions justified on religious grounds and, above all, the primacy of Islamic interpretation. The example of Afghanistan shows where the lines of conflict lie: In an interview, Faisal Ahmad Schinwari, former president of the Supreme Court, told the author[22] that he expected the legal system created at the time of the kingdom to be recognised "within the framework of sharia". Wide-spread implementation of traditional rulings could be expected to follow, and this has been confirmed by events of the past few years. A case in point: following the 2004 elections in Afghanistan a presidential candidate was accused of apostasy by the Supreme Court because he had called for equal rights in divorce for women (cf. Tabeling 2005).

A notable case is that of the Afghan journalist and Islam scholar Ali Muhaqiq Nasab, imprisoned on 1 October 2005 for allowing articles to be published in his magazine Huquq-e zan ("Rights for Women") expressing the views that conversion from Islam did not deserve the death penalty, that flogging for extramarital sexual relations was unacceptable and that Islamic law required men and women to be treated equally. The legal basis for the accusation was Article 31 of the Afghanistan Media Act of 2004 which made it an offence to publish articles "inconsistent with the principles of Islam". After the prosecution had demanded the

---

21 Historically Islam has been remarkably tolerant but its mainstream has not yet resolved the current challenge of equality of rights. In almost all states with Islamic majorities other faiths suffer discrimination to some extent or even persecution, (see current status at www.spiegel.de/panorama/gesellschaft/bild-737920-166803.html, accessed 07.11.12).

22 Comments made in conversation at his official residence on 10.05.2003.

death penalty for apostasy during highly contentious proceedings the journalist was sentenced to two years in prison, against the stated opinion of the Minister for Information and Culture, Rahim, and the commission of enquiry provided for by the Media Act (cf. Wafa / Gall 2005).

A similar recent case concerns the student and journalist Sayed Pervez Kambaksh who had distributed an article on rights for women. Convicted of apostasty in a flawed process by a religious court in the Balkh province of Afghanistan, he was sentenced to death. Initially, the death sentence was confirmed by the Upper House of Parliament but then retracted in the face of international protests. The suspicion is that it was designed to put pressure on his brother, also a journalist, who had exposed many instances of corruption and human rights abuses (cf. Hoskoté/Trojanow 2008, p.13).

This particular case shows how the legally privileged position of Islam is often used in the pursuit of purely secular interests.

In conclusion, it can be said that, in relation to UN standards on human rights, the guarantee of freedom in Islam remains, from a theoretical dogmatic position, largely unresolved. It is all the more interesting to see the emergence of debate and research conducted by Muslims in a constitutional and secular context, separating religious issues from the exercise of political power. Creating the space and institutions for this is one of the more urgent tasks for researchers and politicians. It is gratifying to see this challenge taken up by the Friedrich Alexander University of Erlangen-Nürnberg, which, in 2003, was the first university in Germany to take on the training of teachers of Islamic religion. Now a Department of Islamic Religious Studies has been set up for denomination-oriented teaching and research in accordance with German constitutional law on religion.

References

Badry, Roswitha (1998), *Die zeitgenössische Diskussion um den islamischen Beratungsgedanken (šūrā) unter dem besonderen Aspekt ideengeschichtlicher Kontinuitäten und Diskontinuitäten*, Stuttgart: Franz Steiner Verlag.

Bobzin, Hartmut (2010), *Der Koran. Aus dem Arabischen neu übertragen, unter Mitarbeit von Katharina Bobzin*, Munich: C. H. Beck.

Esfandiari, Golnaz (2005), "Afghanistan editor arrested on blasphemy charges", in: *Straight Goods* 24.10.2005, accessed on 07.11.12 at www.straightgoods.ca/ViewFeature5.cfm?REF=485.

Goldziher, Ignaz (1884), *Die Ẓâhiriten*, Leipzig: Gg Olms.

Hallaq, Wael B. (2005), *The Origins and Evolution of Islamic Law*, Cambridge: Cambridge University Press.

Hoskoté, R. / Trojanow, Ilija (2008), "Den Islam beleidigt", in: *Süddeutsche Zeitung* 16./17.02.2008, p. 13.

Ibn Hišām (1975), *al-sīra al-nabawīya*, vol. 4, ed. Tāhā 'Abdarra'ūf Sa'd, Beirut.

Ibn Khaldūn (1986), *al-muqaddima*, ed. Nasr al-Hūrainī, Beirut.

Jokisch, Benjamin (2007), *Islamic Imperial Law. Harun-Al-Rashid's Codification Project* (Studien Zur Geschichte Und Kultur Des Islamischen Orients), Berlin i.a.: De Gruyter.

Kamali, Mohammad Hashim (1997), *Freedom of Expression in Islam*, Cambridge: Islamic Texts Society.

Kazim, Hasnain (2010), "Christin soll am Galgen sterben", in: *Spiegel-online* 11.11.2010, accessed on 07.11.12 at www.spiegel.de/panorama/gesellschaft/0,1518,728521,00.html.

Krawietz, Birgit (2003), Ibn Taymiyya, Vater des islamischen Fundamentalismus?, in: Atienza, Manuel i.a. (ed.), *Theorie des Rechts und der Gesellschaft: Festschrift für Werner Krawietz zum 70. Geburtstag*, Berlin: Duncker & Humblot, pp. 39ff.

Lucas, Scott C. (2006), The Legal Principles of Muḥammad b. Ismā'īl al-Bukhārī and their Relationship to Classical Salafi Islam, in: *ILAS* 13, No. 3, pp. 289–324.

Melchert, Christopher (1997), *The Formation of the Sunni Schools of Law*, Leiden i.a.: Brill Academic Pub.

Motzki, Harald (1991), *Die Anfänge der islamischen Jurisprudenz. Ihre Entwicklung in Mekka bis zur Mitte des 2./8. Jahrhunderts*, Stuttgart: Harrassowitz.

Muslehuddin, Mohammad (1975), *Islamic jurisprudence and the rule of necessity and need*, Islamabad: Islamic Research Institute.

Peters, Rudolph (2005), *Crime and Punishment in Islamic Law*, Cambridge: Cambridge University Press.

Rohe, Mathias (2011), *Das islamische Recht: Geschichte und Gegenwart.* 3rd edition, Munich: Beck.

Rohe, Mathias (2010), Islam und Menschenrechte. Konfliktlinien und Lösungsansätze, in: Nawrath, Thomas / Hildmann, Philipp W. (eds.), *Interkultureller Dialog und Menschenrechte*, Nordhausen: Bautz, Traugott.

Salqīnī, Ibrāhīm M. (1991), *al-muyassar fī uṣūl al-fiqh al-islāmī*, Beirut/Damaskus: Dar al-Fikr al-Mu'a ṣir.

Tabeling, Petra (2005), "Amnesty Report Afghanistan, Women's Rights only on Paper", *qantara.de* 25.5.2005, accessed 09.02.07 at www.qantara.de/webcom/show_article.php/_c-478/_nr-289/i.html.

Tyan, Emile (1960), *Histoire de l'organisation judiciaire en pays d'Islam*, 2nd edition, Leiden: E.J.Brill.

Wafa, Abdul Waheed / Gall, Carlotta (2005), "Afghan Court Gives Editor 2-Year Term for Blasphemy", in: *New York Times* 24.10.2005.

Wittinger, Michaela (2008), *Christentum, Islam, Recht und Menschenrechte*, Wiesbaden: VS Verlag für Sozialwissenschaften.

wizārat al-auqāf wa l-šu'ūn al-Islāmīya, al-Kuwait, al-mausū'a al-fiqhīya, 4th printing. 1993–2007, vol. 22, pp. 184 ff.

Looking for the positive: Islam in the media

Daniel Meier

1. Introduction

The argument over a proper assessment of Islam is reflected first and foremost in the international mass media. If Islam critics argue, often heatedly, that dialogue with Muslims, including in the mass media, results in the relativising of violence and repression, the complaint by Muslims themselves is above all that the bogeyman image of Islam is a media construct designed to increase circulation at the expense of Muslims. Evaluating the perception of Islam in the media often bears the hallmarks of a proxy fight between, put simplistically, the critics of Islam and Islam sympathisers. More than on any other topic in journalism, a number of empirical studies has appeared in recent years on the topic of news coverage of Islam; considerably more, it should be said, than on the media perception of Christianity, or the Church. By way of example, the present article summarises, in brief, some of the key findings, but does not pretend to give anything like a full overview of research. These findings are then compared with journalists' criteria of perception and the basic functions of journalistic reporting. Finally, recommendations are made for an ethically responsible perception of Islam in journalism. The central focus is on how Islam appears in the media in Germany, supported by sample studies from other European countries. However, the main features and the ethical challenges of media coverage of Islam are very similar throughout Europe.

The analysis of *content*, it should be noted, is only one aspect of more comprehensive processes of communication. Unfortunately, there are, so far as I know, no standard empirical studies which look at the media *communicators* and ask: what are the personal attitudes of journalists and other media professionals towards Islam? What is their basic journalistic intention: is it principally to fulfil a watchdog and alarm function, to meet a self-imposed obligation to alert to threats of terrorism? Or consciously to appeal for sympathy for Muslims? As a guiding principle this is not entirely unproblematic as it conflicts with the requirement that news reporting keeps its distance from its subject. Also, there has been little research to date into the *effect* of news coverage of Islam on media consumers. Nevertheless, according to regular opinion polls, a majority of non-Muslim citizens interviewed in most European countries think that many Muslims are extremists and accuse them of being sympathetic to the use of violence, a finding that can certainly be explained in part by the image of Islam in the media. The effect of these perceptions of Islam is particularly harmful when the reader, listener, viewer or web user has no personal, direct experience of Muslim realities. In concrete terms: when the front cover of a magazine depicts a Muslim flogging himself, covered in blood, and there is no Muslim neighbour, school friend or work colleague in daily life to provide a counter image.

A real issue is that some studies reveal an underlying defensive posture of Islam and indictment of media professionals that goes beyond a systemic critique of the media. This is especially disturbing when judgement is pronounced on "the media" while, on the other hand, journalists are blamed for insufficient differentiation with regard to "Muslims" or "Islam". It makes little sense that journalistic criticism of an actual Islamic terrorist threat should be challenged as merely suggesting a general "unfounded fear of Islam" (Saad 2009, p. 202) due to a preconceived mentality. Lastly, it is irritating when news coverage of Islam which avoids a negative bias in favour of a neutral approach is not interpreted as balanced but as lacking a positive bias, and then criticised for it (see, e.g. Saad 2009, pp. 205ff.). Put more strongly: the supposed ideology-critical rejection of bogeyman images may in itself be an ideology.

2. Journalists' perception of Islam in the light of empirical research: main findings and conclusions

The main thrust of empirical analyses of European media content is that the journalistic connotations or interpretations of Islam are overwhelmingly negative. They show that most themes of violence and conflict, of international terrorism or the oppression of women across the world are linked to Islam, its religion and followers perceived mainly as a threat to security. In contrast, because the presence of Islam in the media is mostly in the context of foreign affairs, normal everyday life receives little attention (for Britain see i.a. Poole 2002, pp. 99ff., pp. 247ff.; for Switzerland see. i.a. Koch 2009). It is also true that the majority of studies limit themselves to foreign journalism and therefore exclude some sympathetic perceptions of Muslim communities in local news media.

In his post-doctoral thesis, Kai Hafez concludes that, chiefly because of the many wars and conflicts during the period concerned, negative event types dominated the perceptions of Islam in reports from foreign correspondents of German daily newspapers (see Hafez 2002, pp. 293ff.). In contrast, even neutral topics, economics for instance, played a secondary role. In a later study commissioned by the German Federal Agency for Civic Education (see Hafez und Richter 2007), Kai Hafez and Carola Richter succeed to their credit in freeing the perception of Islam from foreign news reporting by scrutinising Islam-related material over 18 months in magazine programmes, talk shows, documentaries and special reports from the total output of the two publicly-funded broadcasting stations in Germany, ARD and ZDF. What they found confirms, on the one hand, evidence from the field of Middle East reporting: that themes of terrorism, other acts of violence and the oppression of women constitute 81% of all themes with negative connotations. At the same time they see new, contrasting trends which enable them to give a more nuanced picture on ZDF's "Auslandsjournal" (a German TV series reporting on foreign affairs). In addition to the predominant topic of conflict, new, unfamiliar angles are addressed, a special report on female football fans in Iran, for example, or a report on sex education broadcasts in Egypt.

The British media also show signs of increasing differentiation in the treatment of Islam. Elizabeth Poole, for example, concludes that, "Slippages, ambivalences and contradictions existed in a way that prevented a totalizing, homogeneous Islam. The discourse had multitudinal purposes depending on the variety of issues, priorities and loyalties of different sectors of the press, which varied according to events" (see Poole 2002, p. 185). If one compares European journalists' external perception of political Islam, in particular, with the self-perception of Islam on the Arabic news network Al Jazeera English, they have many points in common (see Schenk 2009, pp. 122ff.), including the fact that peaceful, strongly Islamic countries such as Indonesia are largely ignored. They differ, however, in that Western reporting of terrorism puts a much greater emphasis on the role of the Muslim perpetrators.

Individual studies on selected themes, areas of conflict or groups of people corroborate the empirical findings of a generally negative view of Islam, pointing, for example, to the clearly negative connotations of the theme women and Islam (see Röder 2007). For instance, the picture editors of Germany's leading news magazine "Der Spiegel" worked on contrasting images of veiled Muslim women with negative associations, and modern Muslim women without the veil, focussing in particular on Turkey. The representation of Muslim women, and not only in images, forms a key "frame", that is, a frame of perception for the realities of being Muslim. In this context Khola Maryam Hübsch (see Hübsch 2006) describes the victim frame (the Muslim woman as not free and a submissive victim), the emancipation frame (the Muslim woman as an independent and educated woman), the extremist frame (the Muslim woman as a dangerous fanatic) and also – though rare – the erotic frame (the beautiful Muslim woman, fearful of being flogged). What the analysis of perception framing misses is a "commonality frame" identified by the German weekly "Die Zeit", which relates hijab-wearing Muslim women to Christian nuns, thereby emphasising similarity, and sending a signal of familiarity and normality.

Apart from woman-specific framing, there are other perception frames in the media coverage of Islam which correspond to the journalistic emphasis on conflict and violence already referred to: in the context of the Middle East there are the terrorism frame, the violence frame, and also a David-and-Goliath frame that is actually about Islam, too. What is noticeable in a cross-section of coverage of Islam or the Middle East is the number of metaphors taken from the natural world. When a German report from the Middle East speaks of a "slaughterhouse of the religions"[1] or that on both sides Israelis and Palestinians are "involved in a blood bath"[2], this may be combining underlying elements of an anti-Jewish Christianity with the atavistic idea of a largely Muslim Palestinian people thirsting for blood. Images such as a "wave of violence" or "conflagration" in reports from the Middle East employ metaphors from nature for political events which are, after all, man made, yet implying an inexorable natural force (see Jäger 2003, pp. 352ff.).

In recent years there has been a noticeable trend in several countries for fiction, especially, consciously to present a different point of view contrasting with the sharply negative image of Islam in journalism. The perception of Islam in the mass media swings between fear-inducing and sympathy-seeking, especially in international feature films. "Not Without my Daughter" (1991) is a moving box-office hit portraying Iranian Islamic culture under the influence of American arrogance. The film is based on the autobiography of Betty Mahmoody who accompanied her husband on a short family holiday to his native Persia. He decides not to return to the USA, and his wife desperately attempts to escape with their daughter. Without wishing to question the authenticity of the terrible memories, the film version is a sweeping vilification of devout Muslims, portraying believers as uneducated and primitive, made worse by there being no subtitles for the Persian dialogue. In total contrast, the film of Eric-Emmanuel Schmitt's "Monsieur Ibrahim et les fleurs du Coran" (2003) shows how the individual can attain a state of felicity through Islam. Studiously avoiding explicit religious language, Omar Sharif plays an Arab grocer in Paris whose faith is a vaguely mystical, tolerant Islam. The strangeness of many realities of Muslim life is replaced by his homespun, broadly religious truths about slowness, life and renewal. "I only know what is in my Qu'ran", the shopkeeper keeps repeating as a matter of form. Well, what exactly is that, one is tempted to ask. This wholly unpolitical film

---

1   See "Spiegel", 16.10.2000
2   See "Tagesspiegel", 14.10.2000

makes no attempt at realistically portraying the situation of Muslims living in the French capital; rather, it culminates in a poetic religious fantasy. – This tension between alarmism and partisanship can also be seen in the academic world. Two weighty works published recently in Germany were "Islamfeindlichkeit. Wenn die Grenzen der Kritik verschwimmen" (Schneiders 2010) (Demonisation of Islam. When the boundaries to criticism are blurred), and "Islamverherrlichung. Wenn die Kritik zum Tabu wird" (Schneiders 2010) (Glorification of Islam. When criticism becomes a taboo).

3. Journalistic perception criteria from a professional ethics perspective

Apart from the question of news coverage of Islam, criticism of journalism is often directed at prevailing processes of news selection, picking out in particular the undue emphasis on violence and negativity. By what criteria journalists perceive and evaluate the world is a question which communication research answers in terms of the so-called theory of news values, which identifies certain news factors (see e.g. Maier 2010). The factors of negativity, proximity and consonance are especially relevant in the context of news coverage of Islam, meaning that events, including those concerning Islam, are considered newsworthy because they fit with specific expectations and conform to the world view of media consumers. In this, consonance even outweighs unexpectedness. In other words, a terrorist attack in the Middle East, which can hardly be said to be unexpected in the sense of the maxim, "news is what is different", conforms to expectation. It is rightly emphasised that the roots of these news factors are by no means specific to journalism; most can be interpreted in terms of the psychology of perception as general human interaction values. People's need for novelty and security is more easily satisfied by the unusual and by unrest, by individualisation and personalisation, than by what is normal or peaceful.

Ought the mass media, is the obvious question, to feed such all-too-human needs without restriction, or should their remit not also be to seek new perception criteria? The two pioneers of news values research, Norwegians Johan Galtung and Mari Holmboe Ruge, set out their position clearly in a well-known analysis of newsworthiness ending with the plea, "The policy implications of this article are rather obvious: try to counteract all twelve factors" (Galtung und Ruge 1970, p. 292). It was not the intention of the two researchers who, incidentally, were much involved in peace and conflict research, to provide a kind of recipe book. Rather, in recent media development it has been representatives of the emerging nations callling for a new direction in news production in order to lessen the scope for exclusion and to give a voice to the voiceless, as set out, for example, in the authoritative 1980 MacBride Report for UNESCO:

"[…] The widely-held concept of news values [with] its excessive stress on the departure from the normal […] may inflict on readers and listeners an endless hail of conflicts, catastrophes, crime, natural and man-made disasters, violence, political upheavals, social unrest and economic disorders. […] Catering to the public interest is obviously a valid editorial criterion, yet is it not also reasonable to invest communicators with a certain responsibility to inform the public on matters that ought to concern them and not just appeal to their real or imagined interests? (MacBride 1980, pp. 204ff.).

What media critics forgot, though, is that in a society with free media, the public interest cannot simply be ignored, and news values cannot be introduced, at least in democratic states, through any kind of top-down approach; this used to be the case in communist states, and was – and still is – in many Arab regimes which dictate that one perception criterion must be the achievements of the state. It is true that journalists' understanding of their role in societies undergoing great change is often characterised by conscious partiality for economic and social progress (see Hanitzsch / Seethaler 2009), which may develop into out and out support for the government's policies. In contrast, Western journalists' outrage at attempts by some governments to influence media policy by working together on the sensitive reporting of migration issues may be taken as fundamental scepticism towards any and every intervention by the state. This happened in Germany in 2010 when Aygül Özkan, the minister for social affairs in the Federal State of Lower Saxony, and herself of Turkish origin, proposed a binding "media charter". This was rejected angrily, even though the content of the charter met with the agreement of many media professionals.

Of course, the criticism that religious journalism favours the negativity factor applies to more than just Islam. As a direct result of the revelations of sexual abuse in the past year the Catholic Church has been subjected world wide to news coverage in which violence was the decisive criterion for selection. In that respect, it would be appropriate to exercise restraint, not speaking of *intentional* Islamophobia on the basis of an empirical analysis of *themes* with negative markers, certainly not making comparisons with the defamation of the Jews in the National-Socialist press (see Benz 2011). In my view, what Elizabeth Poole says about the situation in Great Britain could equally well be applied to other journalistic cultures:

"While there was evidence of aversion towards Islam, and overall it was possible to say that coverage was negative, this was just as likely to be a result of journalistic practices and uncritical or conservative modes of thought rather than the malicious intention to discredit Muslims. If the (conscious) defamation of Muslims was the primary objective, coverage, even of these topics, might have been a lot more damning" (Poole 2002, pp. 185ff.).

Political journalism currently faces the challenge of being open and honest about political abuses without deliberately fanning the flames of popular disaffection with politics or democracy. The German political scientist Kurt Sontheimer called it in hindsight a tragic missed opportunity that admirable left-wing social commentators such as Kurt Tucholsky or Carl von Ossietzky did not use their public opposition to the way many felt the Weimar Republic was being perverted in order to lend it their intellectual support (see Sontheimer 1983, p. 305). Against this background many journalists today should ask themselves whether they have not allowed themselves to lose sight of balance in their criticism, with destructive results to the integrity of religious journalism. Of course, the problem cannot be solved through uncritical reporting or by sweeping issues of religion (and associated issues of integration) under the carpet. In these circumstances it is a cause for cautious optimism that in the context of religion journalists are increasingly finding positive angles to events, themes and personalities to report. It is not sufficient simply to say "bad news is good news", and the German sociologist Luhmann is right to speak of success as also being a criterion of perception (see Luhmann 1974, p. 37).

This explains why the perception of real-life integration should not be underestimated as a media value, and why local journalism finds it increasingly newsworthy. There are instances, too, in political journalism where the link between Islam and the "success" factor can be given effective media coverage. A good example of this is the extensive feature on the island nation of the Maldives in the internationally distributed monthly magazine GEO; the cover title in the German edition was: "The Maldives – Islands of optimism. The peaceful transition of an Islamic society" (GEO 5/2011). Also, reporting on Islam could benefit more from the personalisation factor. So it is a matter of real concern that Muslims are often portrayed as a homogeneous, partly threatening and underdeveloped entity. This results in "a collective symbolic coding of Muslims as a violent body of people which has no independent voice and presents a threat to Western societies" (Sonnleitner 2009, p. 199 referring to the Austrian news magazine "profil"). On the other hand, there are signs that journalism is beginning to use individualisation and personalisation in relation to the beliefs and everyday lives of Muslims.

The visualisation factor presents a particular ethical challenge. It is essential that the context of any image should be thoroughly scrutinised. An interesting object lesson is provided by the account of a picture sent in by the French "Agence France-Press" in early February 2006. It showed an Islamic cleric in front of the burning Danish Embassy in Beirut with the text, "Cleric stokes the anger of Muslim faithful in the Lebanese capital", a caption adopted elsewhere, including the German news magazine "Stern", and presumably fitting the consonance factor. The next day the agency issued a correction, which was then correctly published under the same photo by, among others, the "Berliner Zeitung" on 6 February 2006, "Muslim cleric attempts to calm the crowd".

An extremely serious problem for which no obvious solution is in sight is that all the major symbols of Islam, such as mosque, daily prayers, hijab and beard are already seen as Islamist symbols in the minds of the mass media. Mosque, for example, is interpreted less as a place of meeting and prayer, and more as a place of conspiracy. So, for example, when an Islamist terrorist attack is reported, it will be accompanied by a picture of Muslims at prayer. In contrast, the search for symbols to represent Islam less freighted with negative connotations is very difficult. Even the picture of a fashionably-dressed young Turkish Muslim woman is itself a kind of stereotype in that it corresponds too obviously to the "emancipated Muslim woman" frame.

How a journalist chooses perception criteria depends not least on how they view their profession, and that can vary enormously. Put rather crassly, it is the difference between the active, interventionist role and the ideal of the detached observer. Judgements passed, for example, by the German Federal Constitutional Court, describe journalists' functions in ways that can differ widely and be quite contradictory: beside the basic functions of educating and entertaining, there are those of information, criticism, integration, the last being more than just the integration of migrants. The functions of information, criticism and integration, especially, contain the seeds of tension, as when journalists perform their information function as well as their watchdog and alarm functions, yet wish to avoid stirring up anti-Islamic hostility. Media critics such as Kai Hafez, who highlight the need for reporting on migration, now talk of the need for critical reporting of Islam, "It is true that many parts of the Islamic world find themselves in political and social crisis which manifests itself in phenomena of violence. It is also right that social conflicts relating to issues of integration and values must be addressed in the media, because this public space is where solution-oriented action should be prepared." (Hafez 2007, p. 6).

As well as weighing up the public good of collecting and giving information against integration, another major consideration is weighing up freedom of expression against concerns about the possible negative consequences of reporting. The controversy about the ethical legitimacy of publishing the Muhammad cartoons shows that in a case of ethical conflict help can be sought from the traditional, if not clear-cut, distinction between the ethics of values and beliefs, and the ethics of responsibility. To illustrate this dilemma I would like to use an example from my own experience as a journalist. In 2000, as editor of the eastern German "Leipziger Volkszeitung", I was doing some local research into life in a hostel for asylum-seekers in a small town in Saxony. A few days before, during an evening stroll in a Leipzig park, I had met a group of ten young men and women chanting "Sieg Heil", "Foreigners Out" and other slogans. This presented me with the opportunity of adding to my planned piece of journalism some illuminating facts on the miserable situation of Afghan Muslim refugees living in a hostel for asylum-seekers. But the meeting in the hostel proved uncomfortable: the men and women came from well-to-do Afghan homes, had obviously been able to benefit materially from working with the Russian occupation during the Soviet era, and had then fled from the Taliban. Now they complained loudly to me that they had no-one to cook for them and had to clean the toilets themselves. What was I to do? Publish these details in the local newspaper to give readers a realistic picture of the life of Afghan asylum-seekers? Or would the information merely increase the already present xenophobic tendencies of the inhabitants on the basis of, "You see, these people want everything – it's even in the newspaper."? I left out these details, shortening my piece considerably; by doing so, a distinctly distorted slice of real life was reproduced.

4. Conclusion

The German journalist and author Wilhelm Genazino, recipient of the Georg Büchner Prize, once coined the phrase, "the extended gaze". This extended gaze, scrutinising and sympathetic, should, I think, be recommended to journalists for appreciating the mystery of every religion's beliefs. Feature articles and profiles are more suitable journalistic forms than pure news reporting to do justice to the complexity of religious phenomena. Increased public communication about Islam by Muslims could ensure a more nuanced image in the mass media than has been the case up to now. However, from the viewpoint of media and communication ethics, it is not only professional communicators such as journalists and press officers who are responsible for the public face of Islam. In the context of reception ethics consumers also have a responsibility: for example by posting critical feedback to journalism on Web 2.0 sites in the form of blogs or other digital posts, describing their personal experiences of the realities of Muslim life. Admittedly, initial investigations of this "alternative" image of Islam show that such blogs are still much more negative in tone than the professional media. In fact much of the blogosphere contains openly and deliberately Islamophobic sentiments (see e.g. for Austria Lohlker 2009). The sobering conclusion to be drawn is this: instead of the new form of participatory journalism bringing a cautiously hoped-for improvement to the media image of Islam, the blogosphere is often starkly conformist. This is why it makes sense for the media portrayal of Islam to form part of the religious education curriculum, and for students to be taught to explore their own critical approach to the new media between the familiar conflicting demands of freedom and responsibility.

References

Benz, Wolfgang (2011), *Antisemitismus und "Islamkritik", Bilanz und Perspektive*, Berlin: Metropol.

Galtung, Johan / Ruge, Mari Holmboe (1965), The Structure of Foreign News. The Presentation of the Congo, Cuba and Cyprus Crises in Four Foreign Newspapers, in: *Journal of Peace Research* 2, pp. 64–91; cited from Tunstall, Jeremy (ed.) (1970), *Media Sociology. A reader*, London: Constable & Co. Ltd, pp. 259–298.

Genazino, Wilhelm (2006), *Der gedehnte Blick*, München: Deutscher Taschenbuch Verlag.

Hafez, Kai (2002), Das Nahost- und Islambild der deutschen überregionalen Presse, in: Ders., *Die politische Dimension der Auslandsberichterstattung*, vol. 2, Baden-Baden: Nomos.

Hafez, Kai / Richter, Carola (2007), Das Islambild von ARD und ZDF, in: *Aus Politik und Zeitgeschichte*, pp. 26–27. URL: http://www.bpb.de/publikationen/ BSF019.html (accessed: 20.12.2011).

Hanitzsch, Thomas / Seethaler, Josef (2009), Journalismuswelten. Ein Vergleich von Journalismuskulturen in 17 Ländern, in: *Medien und Kommunikationswissenschaften* 4/2009, pp. 464–483.

Hübsch, Khola Maryam (2008), *Der Islam in den Medien. Das Framing bei der Darstellung der muslimischen Frau*, Saarbrücken: Vdm Verlag Dr. Müller.

Jäger, Siegfried & Margarete (2003), *Medienbild Israel. Zwischen Solidarität und Antisemitismus* (MEDIEN –Forschung und Wissenschaft vol. 3), Münster: Lit Verlag.

Koch, Carmen (2009), Das Politische dominiert. Wie Schweizer Medien über Religion berichten, in: *Communicatio Socialis* 4/2009, pp. 365–381.

Lohlker, Rüdiger (2009), Karl Martell verteidigt Wien. Untersuchungen zu islamfeindlichen Blogs in Österreich, in: Bunzl, John / Hafez, Farid (eds.), *Islamophobie in Österreich*, Innsbruck: Studienverlag, pp. 184–190.

Luhmann, Niklas (1974), Öffentliche Meinung, in: Langenbucher, Wolfgang R. (ed.), *Zur Theorie der politischen Kommunikation*, München: Piper Verlag GmbH, pp. 27–54.

MacBride, Sean (1980), *Report of the International Commission for the Study of Communication Problems under the chairmanship of Many Voices, One World – towards a new more just and more efficient world information and communication order*, London / New York / Paris: Rowman & Littlefield Publishers.

Maier, Michaela et al. (2010), *Nachrichtenwerttheorie*, Baden-Baden: Nomos.

Poole, Elizabeth (2002), *Reporting Islam. Media Representations of British Muslims*, London / New York: I. B. Tauris.

Röder, Maria (2007), *Haremsdame, Opfer oder Extremistin? Muslimische Frauen im Nachrichtenmagazin "Der Spiegel"*, Berlin: Frank & Timme.

Saad, Karim (2009), Islamophobie in österreichischen Tageszeitungen, in: Bunzl, John / Hafez, Farid (eds.), *Islamophobie in Österreich*, Innsbruck: Studienverlag, pp. 200–210.

Schenk, Susan (2009), *Das Islambild im internationalen Fernsehen. Ein Vergleich der Nachrichtensender Al Jazeera English, BBC World und CNN International* (Medien und politische Kommunikation – Naher Osten und islamische Welt, vol. 16), Berlin: Frank & Timme.

Schneiders, Thorsten Gerald (2010), *Islamfeindlichkeit. Wenn die Grenzen der Kritik verschwimmen*, 2nd edition, Wiesbaden: VS Verlag für Sozialwissenschaften.

Schneiders, Thorsten Gerald (2010), *Islamverherrlichung. Wenn die Kritik zum Tabu wird*, Wiesbaden: VS Verlag für Sozialwissenschaften.

Sonnleitner, Barbara (2009), Der Karikaturenstreit in den österreichischen Printmedien am Beispiel des Nachrichtenmagazins "profil", in: Bunzl, John / Hafez, Farid (eds.), *Islamophobie in Österreich*, Innsbruck: Studienverlag, pp. 191–199.

Sontheimer, Kurt (1983): Antidemokratisches Denken in der Weimarer Republik. Die politischen Ideen des deutschen Nationalismus zwischen 1918 und 1933, 2nd edition, München: Dtv.

Anti-Semitism and Middle Eastern Media

Peter Philipp

Even Jewish scholars have stated that anti-Semitism was not part of Islam and Islamic society as it has been – and partly still is – in Christian countries and Christian religious circles. Yet, Middle Eastern media frequently publish commentaries, cartoons, "documentaries" and films which are highly reminiscent of anti-Semitic publications in Europe, especially in Nazi Germany or – earlier – in Tsarist Russia. What is therefore called Muslim anti-Semitism in a generalized way has very little to do with the "usual" interpretation of racist anti-Jewish ideology, but it is a Middle Eastern adaptation of European anti-Semitism, mixed with fear and rejection of the old colonial powers and Israel – which is widely looked upon as a "base" of these colonial powers in the Middle East. Anti-Semitism in Middle Eastern media is usually not driven by religious motivation, but the more political Islam is spreading, the more a link is made between religious and political doctrine and feeling also when it comes to anti-Semitic rhetoric.

Rejection of Israel and Antagonism towards Jews

Until the overthrow of Egyptian president Husni Mubarak, the Muslim Brotherhood movement, founded in that country by Hassan Banna in 1928, had been outlawed or at best tolerated for most of its history. Equally, media were not permitted to openly support the brotherhood's program and ideology: namely, that modern Arab states were the creation of the colonial powers' hegemonial interests and policies in the Middle East and that Arab leaders lacked all democratic legitimacy because they depended on foreign powers and their support. The only remedy in the eyes of the Muslim Brethren was Arab unity under the banner of Islam.

Thus, it was not surprising that they also turned against Israel as an "alien element" in the Arab world and became openly hostile towards Jews. Semantically, this was facilitated by the fact that – even today – most Arabs do not use the word "Israelis" but say "Jews" when they refer to the citizens of Israel. They were thereby turning their political antagonism towards Israel into a much more general one against "the Jews", which grew in appeal, becoming common to much larger circles in the Arab world than only the members and followers of the Muslim Brotherhood.

This attitude was also picked up by many of the Arab media, where newspapers often resorted to cartoons and clichés of Jews which closely resembled those of the infamous anti-Semitic Nazi weekly "Der Stürmer". Equally, Arab film and TV productions used these "techniques" in order to reinforce public rejection of Israel. Only in Egypt and Jordan – mainly due to their peace treaties with Israel – did state censorship try to suppress the most virulent examples of anti-Semitic publications. But all too often the authorities simply claimed they had no way to interfere – because the media in their countries were "free and independent".

Arab Spring and new anti-Semitism

In some media (and also political) circles in Egypt, the revolution of 2011 was misunderstood as a green light for unhindered and unlimited expression of hatred against Jews. Surprisingly, for many observers, the Muslim Brotherhood does not ride in the forefront of this development. The success of the revolution (which had come as a surprise to most of the Brethren) had swept them into the role of a leading political power and they realized that they had to strengthen the process of moderation which they had already begun long before the revolution. Otherwise, they would put at risk their first – and perhaps last – opportunity to take over political leadership in Egypt and to reconcile the outside world's suspicions of their movement.

Moderation also meant a different approach to Israel and "the Jews" – much to the displeasure of the Brethren's rank and file. This was the moment of the Salafists – more radical Muslims who consider the Muslim Brotherhood as too lenient, preach "Jihad" against corrupt Arab leaders and reject Israel. Strangely enough, the Salafists had managed to operate various media under Husni Mubarak who seems to have considered them not a danger but a welcome competition to the much bigger and more influential Brotherhood.

Anti-Semitism as a Religious Message

One of their TV stations is "Al Rahma" ("Mercy"), founded in 2007 and owned by the most prominent Salafi preacher, Mohammad Hassan, whose reputation is rapidly spreading across the Arab world, from Morocco to Saudi Arabia. The station is financed by religious Salafists and its program is devoted completely to religious questions and how Muslims should return to the essentials of their religion und the Quran. "Al Rahma's" aim by its own definition is: "To spread the message of Al-Quran and hadith[1] to all human beings in a very effective manner through this channel, so that misgivings and misconceptions about Islam are removed and interfaith trust is re-established in the world"[2].

This includes spreading anti-Jewish slogans and the strengthening of anti-Jewish feelings, if possible by quoting religious texts or even the Quran. One of the "stars" of "Al Rahma TV" is Mohamad Osama, a "child preacher" of elementary school age who recites from the hadith[3]:

"Through worship we shall gain victory over our enemies, strengthen our religion, and defeat the Jews. The Messenger of Allah said: 'Judgement Day will not come before the Muslims fight the Jews, and the Muslims will kill the Jews, and the Jews will hide behind the trees and the stones, and then the trees and the stones will say: Oh Muslim, oh servant of Allah, there is a Jew behind me, come and kill him. Only the gharqad tree[4] will not speak because it is one of the trees of the Jews'."

As hadith, and due to their proximity to the Prophet, such words enjoy protection against criticism. But what about the declarations of individual preachers? A few months earlier[5], preacher Hazem Shuman stated in all clarity what he thought of the Jews: "…these Jews are a cancer. These Jews are a catastrophe. There is not a (single) catastrophe in the world that is not the handiwork of the Jews. These Jews are a cancer in the body of planet Earth, and if permitted, it will spread and infect the entire body. Getting rid of these Jews is a must".

According to Shuman, "the Jews" were responsible for every evil in the world: They had tried to kill the Prophet, they were betraying the Muslims and they were behind the attacks of 9/11. And also their influence on world opinion was not surprising, because… "…today, 92% of the world's film industry is in their hands, 90% of the world's famous actors are Jews, and 90% of the giant news networks, like CNN, are in Jewish hands".

---

1   "Hadith" are accounts of the Prophet's actions, declarations or judgements handed down through the centuries and which are not included in the Quran.
2   http://www.arabic-tvonline.com/2011/12/al-rahma-tv-online-live-watch-channels.html
3   Al Rahma TV, 14. 01. 2012.
4   boxthorn.
5   Al Rahma TV, 09.09.2011.

New Battle and old Arguments

These are expressions and arguments which could stem from the anti-Semitic propaganda machine of the Nazis. Another example was delivered by Gamal Saber, the election manager of one of the disqualified candidates for the Egyptian presidency, Hazem Abu Ismail: He burst out angrily in a TV talk show accusing the anchor woman of being "of Jewish origin", of being paid "a million dollars by Israel" and therefore being so successful in Egyptian TV6. The startled woman told him to leave the studio insisting that he had offended her by calling her "Jewish" (which she is not).

Although these were examples of anti-Semitic language by Islamists in the Egyptian media, even the non-religious channels are not free of this: Privately owned "Tahrir TV" was the first new station to start after the outbreak of the revolution and it operates under the motto "the people want to liberate their minds". One way of doing so is by "enlightening" the Egyptian public about the evil character of the Jews: "Tahrir TV" has been re-broadcasting "Horseman without a Horse" – a series which already caused international uproar in 2002 because of its blatant anti-Semitic bias and was consequently taken off the air.

The show depicts meetings of Jewish leaders who plan to take over the world – in clear resemblance to the "Protocols of the Elders of Zion"[7], a text originating in Tsarist Russia and hence used by anti-Semites in many countries, including the US. In addition to the dramatization of this story, the audience is presented with "expert" explanations – as if this was based on serious and scientific research.

Satellite Technology Spreads the Word

Muslim preachers play an important role in the propagation of such texts and theories. Before the age of satellite TV, the impact of their speeches and sermons was limited to local audiences. Today, the availability of relatively cheap air time and satellite receivers throughout the Arab and Muslim worlds makes it easy to spread their word not only into the most secluded parts of each country but also across borders and from one continent to another.

---

6   Al-Mehwar TV, 17.04.2012.
7   The "Protocols of the Elders of Zion" were first published in Russia in 1903 and by now have been translated into many other languages. As the claimed protocol of subversive activities and meetings of "World Jewry" on its way to take control of world economy, the media and eventually political power, this publication served the Nazis as an important justification for the Holocaust.

The introduction of inter-Arab and Arab international satellite broadcasting, pushed forward especially since the start of "Al Jazeera TV" on Nov 1st 1996, is rightly considered the opening of a new era of free access to information in a region which had until then suffered from local censorship and state control of the news. At the same time, however, new and ideologically orientated satellite stations started to broadcast their programs throughout the Arab world and beyond. In this, "ideology" mainly stands for a mix of religious and political theories and arguments, such as religiously motivated rejection of the US and, consequently, of their "foothold" in the Middle East – Israel – and "the Jews".

A TV station pushing this to perfection is "Al Manar"[8], privately owned but closely affiliated to the Lebanese Shiite movement of "Hezbollah"[9] ("Party of God") and broadcasting from Beirut. Arabsat[10] is the largest shareholder (36%) and it is through their channels that "Al Manar" reaches Arab viewers throughout the Arab world, Europe and beyond.

The proximity between "Al Manar" and "Hezbollah" but mainly the content of its program put an end to the station's attempt to reach Arabs in Europe through satellites of the Paris-based company "Eutelsat": After four years of broadcasting via Eutelsat, the Supreme Administrative Court of France ("Conseil d'État") ruled at the end of 2004 that Eutelsat had to withdraw the license for "Al Manar" because the station was broadcasting anti-Jewish and anti-Semitic programs. Among them was the above-mentioned "Horseman without a Horse", but also the allegation that Jews ("the Zionists") had spread AIDS in the Arab world.

Copying European Models

Such examples of open anti-Semitism are relatively new for the Arab and Islamic world. Although Prophet Mohammed is known to have cursed the Jews openly for not being willing to abandon their belief and to convert[11], Islam has

---

8   In English: "the lighthouse".

9   Hezbollah – "Party of God": A militant Shiite movement founded in 1982. Open hostility with Israel which repeatedly led to armed clashes and even open war (2006). Being openly supported by Iran and Syria, "Hezbollah" has been listed as a terrorist organization by the US in 1999. Neither the EU nor the UN have followed this step but maintain a very critical position towards Hezbollah which has meanwhile become a political party and a dominant factor in the government of Lebanon.

10   Arabsat is the Arab League's satellite communications organization, established in 1976. Their satellites cover not only the Arab world but also reach into Europe and – through different pay-TV companies – they can be viewed world-wide – with an estimated viewership of 50 million.

11   For example in Sura 5:60 "Should I inform you of those, who will have even worse recompense from Allah than the transgressors? They are those whom Allah has cursed. Who have been un-

treated Jews and Christians most of the time as "people of the Book" and as "dhimmis" – members of minorities for whom the Muslim state carries a special responsibility. The most famous, productive and fruitful example of peaceful co-existence and cooperation was undoubtedly Muslim rule over "El Andalus" (Andalusia).

The lack of anti-Jewish stereotypes in the Muslim world came to an end with the rise of Jewish immigration to Palestine, the establishment of Israel as "the Jewish state" and growing support for it especially from Western countries. As if they had been in a rush to find "appropriate" enemy-pictures, Arab media – especially their caricaturists cartoonists – began to draw from examples the Nazi propagandists had produced in abundance.

This explains why Jews in most Arab and Muslim cartoons were – and still are – depicted as "Hassidic" East European Jews – with long black coats, black hats and beards. This is a stereotype of Jews that had not been known to the Middle East and also was – and still is – unrepresentative of the inhabitants and citizens of Israel. But it was this type of a Jew that had dominated anti-Semitic cartoons in Nazi Germany and in other countries outside the Middle East. Ironically, it was mainly members of the Christian minority who introduced these Nazi-style clichés: They had been exposed to the anti-Semitic approaches of their Church education and they also frequently behaved more nationalistically than the mainstream Muslim population – in order to prove their loyalty to the "common Arab cause"[12].

Anti-Jewish allegations were and still are also taken from anti-Semitic tales of the past: Medieval Jews, for example, were slurred of ritual killings of Christian children and of drinking their blood. The same picture reappeared in the preface to a best-selling book, published in the 1980s and for which former Syrian minister of defence, Mustafa Tlas[13] had written at least the preface. Similar claims and accounts have appeared before and after this on numerous occasions in Arab newspapers and other media and they all follow a pattern used by anti-Semitic

---

der His wrath. Some of whom were turned into apes and swine. Who worshipped taghut (idols). Those are the people who are in a far worse plight and who have turned farthest away from the Right Way."

12   e.g. "Semites and Antisemites", New York/London: Norton, 1986, by Bernard Lewis, or "Muslim Attitudes to Jews and Israel: The Ambivalences of Rejection", Sussex Academic Press, 2010, edited by Moshe Ma'oz.

13   The book, "The Matzoh of Zion," refers to an incident in Damascus where in 1840 a Christian priest disappeared and was said to have been victim of ritual killing by Jews who used his blood for the preparation of "matzoh" – the unleavened bread served for Passover. When the book appeared in 1984, this led to a deterioration of the strained relations between Syria and the US and other Western countries. Damascus rejected Washington's accusation/charge of anti-Semitism: Syria was against "Zionism", but not against "the Jews".

circles in Tsarist Russia. Tlas justified and defended the book as the "Muslim an-swer to Schindler's List'".

World Conspiracy – from the Tsar to 9/11

The close link between political rejection of Israel and expressed through anti-Semitic rhetoric is all too obvious. For decades – and subconsciously perhaps even today, Arab public opinion has been unable to understand the fact that the small State of Israel had again and again been able to defeat combined Arab armed forces or had survived wars with them. The only explanation they could come up with was that Israel was not only supported by Western powers – like the United States – but it also managed to force upon them its political agenda: The old dream to subdue first the Arab and Muslim and then the rest of the world.

A conspiracy theory par excellence, supported through the centuries by simi-lar theories in Europe and circulated again since 9/11: Arab and Muslim media are particularly amenable to the theory that the attack on the World Trade Center was not carried out by Muslims but by agents of the Israeli Mossad[14]. As "proof" of this theory totally unfounded reports are circulating that Jews working in the WTC on Sept 11th were told to stay away on that day[15]. The reasoning behind the 9/11 conspiracy: Israel wanted to win over George W. Bush for its fight against Muslims and Arabs. In fact, Bush had been one of Israel's staunchest supporters already before 9/11 and Israel hardly needed any drastic action to make him an ally[16].

Of Semites and anti-Semites

From most of these examples it becomes obvious that anti-Semitic rhetoric in the Arab media is not hard-core racism like the Nazis used to produce, but a mixture

---

14   Mossad – Israeli intelligence service, specializing in international operations.
15   There are no reliable figures for the religious affiliation of the victims, but most attempts to find out how many of them were Jewish result in a figure of around 300 or roughly 10 %.
16   Most of these far-fetched theories – by members of the "truth movement" – originate in the US and in European countries but have been widely circulated throughout the Arab und Muslim worlds and taken at face value there. One of these conspiracy theories was written by a former secretary of state in the German ministry of defence, Andreas von Bülow: "The CIA and September 11" and found wide acceptance throughout the Middle East and beyond. Another player has been Iranian president Mahmoud Ahmadinejad who in his speech at the UN on Sept 23rd 2010 blamed "certain elements in the US administration" for 9/11.

of political arguments emanating from the Israel-Palestine conflict and the attempt to explain and overcome an inferiority complex versus the former colonial powers and Israel. And it is – to quite an extent – the expression of suspicion towards the real intentions of these powers.

Confronted with the similarity of racist anti-Semitic rhetoric and vocabulary to that used against "Jews" in the media and public life of today's Arab world, the reaction is usually the same: How could Arabs be anti-Semites – since they are themselves Semites? Also the definition of "anti-Jewish" will not be accepted. The most prominent preacher in the Sunni-Muslim world, Yusuf Al-Qaradawi, justified staying away from an interfaith conference in Qatar with Jewish participants by arguing that he had nothing against Jews, only against "Zionists"; and that he had already met on repeated occasions with members of the Neturei Karta[17] movement[18].

Arab countries – and consequently also their media – vary in their official attitude towards Jews: Egypt, Tunisia and Morocco have Jewish communities, synagogues and a certain amount of Jewish community life under official protection of by the state. Other countries – like Jordan – never had a Jewish minority and the third group – among them Yemen, Syria, Lebanon and Iraq – once had thriving Jewish communities of which all but a few members have gone to Israel or other countries. In none of these countries can one find official anti-Semitic or anti-Jewish legislation. Restrictions stem however from the latent tension between these countries and Israel and the constant suspicion brought against Jews as possible agents of Israel.

Iran – A special Case?

A classic but also in many ways different case is the Islamic Republic of Iran. It has so far not been dealt with here because Iran is not an Arab country and the vast majority of its citizens are Shiite Muslims. Until the fall of the Shah's re-

---

17   Neturei Karta (from Aramaic "Guardians of the City") – an ultra-orthodox Jewish group based mainly in the US and with a small minority in Israel – that rejects the state of Israel. They believe that the "Jewish State" will be established by God only when the Messiah comes. They reject the creation of Israel as a blasphemous act because it pre-empts divine prophecy.

18   http://www.dailystar.com.lb/ArticlePrint.aspx?id=66735&mode=print
"some Muslim and Christian figures had opted to stay away from the conference 'because they do not favor conducting a dialogue with the Jews coming from Israel'." They include the Egyptian-born Qaradawi, "who is consistent with himself – when he and other Muslim and Christian religious figures say they will not talk with the Jews, they do not mean Jews in the absolute/in general".

gime in 1979, Tehran and Jerusalem entertained close relations with intense co-operation in a wide scope of issues – among them predominantly security matters – and Iran was Israel's major supplier of oil. Because of their affiliation with the Shah, the US and Israel turned into the new rulers' principal enemies: Since the revolution Israel has been called the "little Satan" by Tehran's religious rulers – the "big Satan" being the United States.

This denunciation has been widely used by the Iranian media, while the roughly 25,000 Jews who stayed in Iran[19] after the revolution and who constitute the largest Jewish community in the Middle East outside Israel, enjoy relative freedom as a recognized and protected minority with clearly defined rights. For example, they are entitled to one seat in parliament ("majles"), they have their own synagogues (16 of them in Tehran but also in other parts of the country), they run their own schools and a renowned charity hospital. After years of travel restrictions, they can now even go and visit relatives in Israel and some of those have come to visit their kin in Iran.

The revolutionary leader of 1979, Ayatollah Khomeini, instructed the new government to give Jews (and Christians) the protected status as "dhimmi". The Iranian media seem to forget, however, what this means: Very often they are critical of "the Jews" when they mean Israel and in times of unrest they support collective suspicion against Iranian Jews: In 1998/9 thirteen Jews were arrested in Shiraz on the claim they were spying on behalf of Israel. After a long trial they were sentenced to long prison terms. For the media, their "guilt" had been beyond any doubt from the outset.

Jews and Zionists

Iranian State officials practise a different approach and make sure that this is published by the media: The name of "Israel" is hardly ever used, but that of "the Zionists" or – together with the US – "Satan" and the "World Arrogance". To prove that this had nothing to do with animosity towards Jews, the Iranian authorities demonstratively entertain contact with "non-Zionist" Jewish groups from abroad – especially the "Neturei Karta"[20]. This was the case in 2007, when a conference was convened in Tehran about "The World without Zionism". The

---

19   The Iranian Jewish population rose from approximately 35,000 in 1900 to almost 150,000 in
      1948. In that year, the State of Israel was declared and emigration to Israel reduced the number
      of Iranian Jews to around 80,000 on the eve of the revolution (1979). Since then, is has declined
      again – to approximately 25,000, but is still the largest Jewish community in a Muslim country

20   See footnote 15.

Iranian media widely published the proceedings of this conference, stressing – especially in foreign language reports – that this was not an anti-Jewish event. Photos of President Mahmoud Ahmadinejad receiving the "Neturei Karta" delegation were prominently displayed.

The conference was not the first and not the last occasion that Ahmadinejad drew international criticism of his and his government's attitude towards Jews. More than his predecessors, this president has repeatedly provoked with public statements about Israel, the Jews and the Holocaust that were published in the Iranian media and often left room for interpretation, but were internationally understood as anti-Jewish and anti-Semitic.

"An Insult to all the World's Jewish Communities"

Shortly after his first election, Ahmadinejad quoted Ayatollah Khomeini that "Israel would disappear from the map". (This has since been published abroad as Ahmadinajad's own appeal to destroy Israel). Ahmadinejad supported a Tehran daily's ("Hamshahri") call for a competition of cartoons about the Holocaust and he started questioning the Holocaust by claiming there was no scientific research about it. It only served the Zionists to obtain world support. This – at least indirect – denial of the Holocaust caused an international uproar, but also criticism from the Jewish member of parliament at the time, Maurice Motamed[21], who declared in an interview with "Radio Farda", the Persian service of the Voice of America: "Denial of such a great historical tragedy that is connected to the Jewish community can only be considered an insult to all the world's Jewish communities"[22]. Another Jewish leader and head of the Jewish community at the time, Haroun Yashayaei, complained in 2006 directly to Ahmadinejad about calling the Holocaust "a myth" at a "Holocaust Conference" staged in Tehran. In a letter to the president he describes the Holocaust as one of the most obvious and saddest events of the 20th century: "How is it possible to ignore all the undeniable evidence existing for the killing and exile of the Jews in Europe during World War II?"[23].

---

21 Motamed was twice elected to the majlis – in 2000 and 2004.
22 http://www.rferl.org/content/article/1342577.html
23 http://www.rferl.org/content/article/1342577.html
    http://www.spiegel.de/international/spiegel/0,1518,455172,00.html

"We love everyone in the world"

Such open criticism of Iranian political leaders by members of the Jewish community is rare. It shows, however, that they do have some room for free expression. Ahmadinejad's reaction was also surprising: He donated money for the Jewish hospital and declared, while at the UN in 2006, that he was not anti-Jewish: "We love everyone in the world – Jews, Christians, Muslims, non-Muslims, non-Jews, non-Christians... We are against occupation, aggression, killings and displacing people – otherwise we have no problem with ordinary people".[24]

Speeches and actions of the Iranian president are repeated in the Iranian printed media which are under tight government control and easily risk losing their license. Radio and TV, which broadcast on numerous channels, offer even less variety because they are state-run. Iranian TV has repeatedly aired anti-Israeli films in which the Jews were depicted as in anti-Semitic cartoons. But then, Iranian TV also produced and ran "Zero Degree Turn" – a series about a young Iranian diplomat in Paris saving Jews from Nazi-deportation and death.

This program was shown only months after Ahmadinejad's claims about the Holocaust and added to the irritation about the attitude of Iran and its media towards Jews.

Israel – The Case is Clear

For Israel, such irritation never existed: Israeli media and Israeli politicians are convinced that the Iranian leadership is using anti-Semitic rhetoric out of conviction and that even ambiguous declarations against Israel derive from such anti-Semitic motivation and have to be taken at face value. This basic feeling has been contributing to the escalation of the conflict about the Iranian nuclear program during the past ten years: Israel is convinced that the leadership of the Islamic Republic wants to "get rid" of Israel sooner or later. And the more Israel, Israelis and Jews are demonized in the Iranian media (and by Iranian politicians) the more the Iranian public might start to accept such an idea.

Anti-Semitic publications in Arab media seem to be viewed in a different way by Israel. To many Israelis they serve as justification for the old suspicion and claim that "the Arabs" were not ready to live in peace with Israel – even in the cases of Jordan and Egypt with which Israel has signed peace treaties. This strengthens nationalistic tendencies in Israel against concessions and eventually

---

24   http://news.bbc.co.uk/2/hi/middle_east/5368458.stm

more peace treaties with other Arabs. And it affects the core of the Middle East conflict – the Israeli-Palestinian problem. Liberal Israelis know and warn that this is a vicious circle: The longer the Palestine problem remains unsolved, the more antagonism against Israel will spread throughout the Arab and Muslim World and this again will harden the Israeli position.

Psychologically understandable

Such views are not popular in Israel and Jewish authors who publish such ideas are quickly slurred as "self-hating Jews" while non-Jewish writers face the accusation of being anti-Semitic. In view of Jewish history and the Holocaust such a reaction and sensitivity may be psychologically understandable, but it also weighs heavily on the attempts to find a peaceful solution for the Middle East and it is a growing burden on Israel's foreign relations: International solidarity as in the case of the Iranian nuclear program might not last forever.

German media have a Problem

One country deeply affected is Germany. It has long developed into one of Israel's staunchest allies but it lacks the power to give the peace-process the necessary impetus. The German chancellor, Angela Merkel, stated in her speech in the Knesset in March 2008, that Israel's security was not negotiable for Germany, but that is not the point, because nobody wants to negotiate Israel's security. German politicians support Israel, but they know that the growing hard line attitude in Israel is making this very difficult.

German politicians treat Israel with velvet gloves, but the media do criticize Israel's occupation policy and its position towards the question of a Palestinian state. When, however, they cast doubt on the Israeli arguments about the Iranian nuclear program, they are quickly attacked by self-styled defenders of Israel who scan the media for critical remarks which they can use to construct an anti-Semitic attitude. Mainstream media are not so much affected by this because they are more hesitant to be critical towards Israel and Jews. This already starts when it comes to the use of the word "Jew" – as if this was a pejorative expression.

When it comes to individual voices of criticism, however, they are exposed to the full power of "anti-Racist rejection". The latest one to be exposed to this was German Nobel Prize laureate Günter Grass: In a "poem" which was far from

62

Grass's artistic level and showed a number of factual mistakes, he criticized Israel for its threat to attack Iran. Immediately some – and later many – German media attacked the writer for having acted out of anti-Semitic motives. Israel (over)reacted a few days later by declaring Grass "persona non grata". Eighty-four-year-old Grass in turn attacked the media for launching a campaign against him. It took some more days until sober observers came to the conclusion that Grass was no anti-Semite and the media had not campaigned against him. But the case showed that the German media have a problem with German past, the Holocaust, Jews and Israel. However, one thing may be said: They are anything but anti-Semitic.

Dangerous Indoctrination

After centuries of peaceful coexistence between Muslims, Christians and Jews in the Middle East, the proclamation of the State of Israel in 1948 and its preparation during the preceding decades can be seen as the start of a kind of Middle Eastern anti-Semitism which draws from political rejection of Israel, from religious quotes in Hadith and Quran and also European anti-Semitic textbooks. Muslim politicians in the Arab world and in Iran are using this language and their media are multiplying it. So are certain Muslim preachers, and the general public in these countries is exposed to massive indoctrination against „the Jews".

This has a negative effect not only in the Muslim countries of the Middle East, but also in Israel where it is seen as proof that the Muslim world was not ready for peace with Israel and that it was basically anti-Semitic. It also has a negative effect on European and other countries where these arguments are being picked up by certain political groups and elements: Some of them condemn any form of criticism of Israel as anti-Semitism, others use them as an instrument to show that the victims (of the Holocaust) have long become culprits themselves – namely Israel as an occupying power.

References

Lewis, Bernhard (1998), Muslim Anti-Semitism, in: *Middle East Quarterly*, pp. 43–49.
Lewis, Bernhard (1986), *Semites and Antisemites*, New York/London: Norton.
Moshe Ma'oz (2010), *Muslim Attitudes to Jews and Israel. The Ambivalences of Rejection*, Eastbourne: Sussex Academic Press.

The presence of religious peace initiatives in the media

Markus A. Weingardt

Religious peace initiatives – some examples

On the 27 June 2010 the first free elections for more than 50 years were held in West African Guinea. Voter turnout was high and the process largely peaceful. These elections and the preceding peace agreement were widely reported in the media, on radio and television. What was *not* reported was that the Catholic lay Community of Sant'Egidio had played a significant, even leading role in negotiating this peace agreement which was signed at the Community's office in Rome on 28 May 2010.[1]

After decades of violence, dictatorship, civil war, repression and massacres, a peace treaty was surely worthy of media attention. The Community of Sant'Egidio is, after all, not unknown: its representatives had already brokered a peace accord in 1992 ending the brutal 15-year civil war in Mozambique, which earned it the sobriquet of the "UN of Rome" (Boutros Boutros-Ghali) and inspired it to act as mediator in several other conflicts around the globe: in states such as Burundi and Guatemala, Algeria and Albania (cf. Weingardt 2010, pp. 137–158). Yet the German media did not consider the success of an explicitly religious peace actor in Guinea worthy of report; it was literally *not worth mentioning* (the success owed, incidentally, to a Christian group in a country that is 90% Muslim!).

But this is not an isolated case. Who has heard of the movement for peace and reconciliation started by the Buddhist monk Maha Ghosananda in *Cambodia* after the Khmer Rouge reign of terror – an exemplary, pioneering movement over thirty years to develop civil society in this damaged, divided country? Who knows of the mediation efforts and non-violence fatwas of Grand Ayatollah Ali al-Sistani, one of the most senior and influential Shiite clerics, in *Iraq* (2004/05)? Why are there no reports of peace work by the *Interreligious Councils* and their initiatives in *Sierra Leone*, *Liberia*, *Uganda* and *Sri Lanka* or in former *Yugoslavia*? These are no pleasant round-table discussions, but initiatives which, often at the highest political level, had, and still have, a significant influence in shaping the peaceful development of those countries! Who remembers that in the Beagle

---

1   This *Accord Politique Global* was signed by 21 leading politicians and representatives of civil society as well as by Mario Giro, who mediated for Sant'Egidio, (cf. Seiterich 2010, p. 21).

conflict the unpredictable escalation between *Argentina and Chile* was only averted at the eleventh hour by the intervention of Pope John Paul II, and that years of mediation by the Vatican finally led in 1984 to the Treaty of Peace and Friendship between the two countries which finally brought the century-old dispute to an end? Why, in none of the news reports or publications on "Islam and violence" or "Islam and non-violence", is there anything on the one ethnic group that opposed violence in the 1994 genocide in *Rwanda*, namely the Rwandan Muslims? Not only had they – on specifically *religious* grounds – refused to participate in violence, but, as attested by Christian Scherrer, special investigator for the UN, (cf. Scherrer 1995), they had given substantial support to refugees and those in distress, regardless of tribal allegiance or religious belief. Why was the role of the church in the East German *Wende* given little coverage in reports of the celebrations for the twentieth anniversary of German reunification; as little, in fact, as for the twentieth anniversary of the fall of the Berlin Wall just one year earlier? Yet it was undoubtedly the Christian churches in East Germany which – together with the then Soviet head of State Mikhail Gorbachev – ensured the peaceful dismantling of that political system.

This brief outline is confirmed by large-scale surveys which conclude that the contribution of faith-based actors in the peace-making process tends to be ignored or marginalised by the media, which concentrate entirely on the potential in religions for inciting conflict and violence. Regrettably, there is indeed much that can be reported about this. But the generalisation into an overall impression is false, a distortion of reality: religions are not *exclusively* dangerous, exacerbating, even inciting violence. Faith-based actors – individuals, communities, initiatives, movements – are just as capable of *defusing* conflict, that is: making peace.

As the previous examples show, they can do so, and have been doing so for many years. Eminent examples are Mahatma Gandhi, Martin Luther King and the current Dalai Lama: all highly political actors and, at the same time, deeply religious individuals. Throughout the world they are seen as *the* heroes of non-violent conflict transformation – as unique, singular phenomena. Scarcely anyone cares a jot about their many "brothers and sisters" whose work, even leading to martyrdom, is just as significant.

The marginalisation of faith-based peace initiatives in the media

Exceptions apart, what can explain the fact that the media ignore or marginalise faith-based peace initiatives? The reasons are many and complex, but four possible causes are suggested here:

1. Implicitly or explicitly, media reporting, correspondents and news agencies pursue *political intentions*; therefore, reports deemed unhelpful to these intentions are suppressed. It is scarcely conceivable that the Rwandan Muslims' refusal to participate in violence in 1994 should go unnoticed, especially after the UN special investigator's report and, above all, in the wake of the 100 days' massacre. The same can be said of Ali al-Sistani's efforts at mediation and his fatwas calling on all Iraqis to renounce violence. It can only be assumed that this was simply not the image of Islam many people had. But instead of correcting the image, news reporting was skewed – with disastrous consequences for the shaping of social and political opinion, in Europe and beyond.

2. Many of those working in the media and the major news agencies belong to a generation for whom, *personally, religion plays a marginal role, or no role at all*, and who probably encountered few religious concepts during their professional training in the 1970s and '80s. At that time the theory of secularisation, the belief that religion would shortly become obsolete and socially and politically irrelevant, was at its height. This did not happen, and religion is said (even if with equal overstatement) to have made a comeback, even undergone a renaissance, on the political scene, a fact greeted by some with *astonishment*, by others with *total* indifference. The latter, perhaps subconsciously and without malice, continue to consider religion as irrelevant in peace making, even when the opposite is plain to see, as in Guinea.

3. Another reason for this lack of interest is that working for peace does not create headlines, is not *sensational*, especially the innumerable small-scale local initiatives. Peace building and conflict mediation, especially when faith-based, usually – and deliberately – take place quietly, behind the scenes, at least until negotiations are concluded. Such work is long and hard, demanding in the extreme, yet appears unspectacular. Peace is not considered as "sensational", therefore not newsworthy – unlike war and violence. The saying "when it bleeds, it leads" still dominates news reporting, often succinctly expressed (the economic argument is not far away) as, "Bad news, conflict, violent extremes and clashes, are what the reader – or viewer – wants and demands".

4. In addition, religious peace making is marginalised in the media, because it is marginalised by *politics, society* and the *academic community* – even by the *religious communities themselves. Politics* rarely acknowledges the peace potential of religious communities, rarely takes account of their peace-making activities. *Society* is dominated by a biased, distorted image of religion as violent, an image vigorously promoted by many of the media. The *academic community*, in particular peace and conflict research, has long ignored religion as irrelevant in (peace) policy making before – following Huntington's theory of the clash of civilisations – attacking its potential for violence. Only gradually has the aware-

ness grown that de-escalation and peace making are part of the ambivalence of religion. Also, the *religious communities* of all denominations, though emphasising that peace is at the heart of their doctrine, in actual fact relegate peace making to a subordinate role. The amount of peace building (in its widest sense) undertaken in and by religious communities throughout the world is remarkable. Nevertheless, "peace" is not at the top of the agenda (with the exception of the historic peace churches). In the 1980s the Christian churches in Germany were still the driving force of the peace movement, but for ordinary church members and officials peace making is no longer as important now as it was then; neither memoranda nor pastoral letters can hide that fact. When religious peace efforts are of such limited interest in all spheres of politics and society it is hardly to be wondered at if this resonates with, and is reflected in, the media.

Conclusion: What can be done?

What can we conclude from this evidence? The enormous social and political influence of the media is undeniable. The marginalisation of religious peace initiatives by the media, however, may certainly be disputed, not accepted as a law of nature. Indeed, the opposite is true: the media is a force to be used positively and presents a huge challenge for our time. As already shown, religious resources for peace making have been ignored or marginalised not just by the media, but also by politics, academic and religious communities, and they, too, must meet this challenge

1. As already stated, the *academic community* is gradually acknowledging that the potential for promoting peace is inherent in the ambivalence of religion. The task now is to translate this into research projects, with established researchers to promote awareness and understanding among the next generation of researchers. Students of the post-9/11 era have grown up with an entirely different experience of the political relevance of religion – which can be an advantage. However, the success of every research project is dependent on research funding, and this requires funding institutions – scholarship programmes, the research foundations, and the like – to be open to religious aspects of peace research. The German Foundation for Peace Research has set a good example over a number of years. However, many funding agencies have yet to rethink their policies on this and give appropriate regard to the role of religious communities in shaping peace policy. It is encouraging that recently, the importance of their role has been amply demonstrated in a number of studies currently available. (cf. Sampson 1997, Hasenclever 2003, Basedau/Körner 2009, Appleby 2000, Weingardt 2010, Little

2007) The issue only needs to be taken up by the academic community and published material will follow; the media will then have no option but to report.

2. Challenges facing *politics*: even politicians are not immune to media reports and pictures, especially not when presented as the "voice of the people". Many people in positions of political responsibility hold to the media's distorted image of religion, and do not recognise that religions can contribute to conflict resolution. The thinking is, rather, that violent conflict can only be ended through violence. This is illustrated by some patronising reactions to comments on Afghanistan made by Margot Käßmann, the then Chair of the Council of the Evangelical Church in Germany. In her New Year's Day sermon in 2010 she called for a more "imaginative" approach in dealing with conflict, and referred to the successes of faith-based peace actors (Cf. Käßmann 2010). The reactions of politicians ranged from accusations of naivety to ridicule. She was invited to "sit down in a tent with the Taliban and [...] prepare rituals with them with candles and prayers" (Reinhold Robbe, SPD, at the time, German parliamentary commisssioner for the armed forces, cited in: Fischer/Gathmann 2010). Comments like these reveal the limited understanding, not of Frau Käßmann, but of those making them. In their own interests and those of peace, politicians would do well to take notice of religious peace workers, and to take them seriously. Faith-based peace actors should be identified, encouraged and supported – not taken over! – and involved intelligently in emergency peace processes: as mediators or advisers, either in the public eye or discreetly in the background. There are many examples to show how much can be achieved.

Politicians could also provide more political backing and financial resources to civil peace work in which there are many faith-based groups and organisations. A start was made in 2004 with the German government's Action Plan "Civilian Crisis Prevention, Conflict Resolution and Post-Conflict Peace-Building". 30 million euros were set aside for this, though a drop in the ocean when compared with a defence budget of 30 billion euros. Politicians, even more than the academic community, should know that if they involve religious peace workers more, *ask* more of them, and engage their commitment, then increased reporting by the media will follow.

3. What challenges do the *religious communities* face if they are to reverse the marginalisation of faith-based peace efforts? First, peace must become a top priority in parishes, on boards and in the pulpit. Practical, active support for peace building through financial and human resources currently lags far behind what is widely acknowledged as the immense worth theologically. Then there needs to be strong public relations activity presenting the work churches and other religious communities do for peace more clearly. Even if the secular media find little to report, the religious communities should at least restore the balance in their

own publications. There has been some movement in this direction, but not nearly enough to make peace a fundamental core priority. Finally, the religious communities – not just the usual funding agencies – could encourage a reappraisal of their potential for peace through research and journalistic activity. This is not just about awareness raising and public relations; it is a prerequisite if others are to gain from these experiences and develop existing skills and resources.

4. Finally, of course, there is the challenge to the *media*. The old journalists' motto is "to inform and to enlighten". There is definitely no lack of reporting when religion contributes to escalating conflict; but there certainly is when the outcome is *de*-escalation. This is spelled out in a study by the German Institute for Global and Area Studies (GIGA) in Hamburg which examines the role played by religious communities in 28 recent violent conflicts in Sub-Saharan Africa (cf. Basedau/Körner 2009). The study comes to the conclusion that in 19 of these conflicts the religious communities did contribute to an escalation of violence; events, for example, in Uganda, Sudan, Somalia and Nigeria have been, and are, given extensive coverage. However, the study also shows that in these 19 and a further 6, that is, in 25 of the 28 conflicts, faith-based actors contributed significantly to *de-escalation*. The fact that there were more religious resources devoted to peace is in striking contrast to the media emphasis on the contribution of faith-based actors in Africa to conflict escalation.

"To inform and to enlighten" does mean not ignoring circumstances where religion incites violence. It is right that it should be reported, and not played down or concealed. But the *Peace Counts* project shows how things can be different. Professional journalists and photographers joined forces precisely to report on successful *peace initiatives* around the world – not only about, but including faith-based actors. The outcome has been an award-winning reportage, which both informs and enlightens, on those aspects of conflict which are usually ignored. This is investigative journalism in the best sense.

It is my hope that when the peace potential of faith-based actors is given due recognition by the academic community, politicians and religious communities, then the media will have no option but to deal with it properly, or at least more explicitly. Naturally, reference to "the media" does not apply to all equally; there are notable exceptions among organs of the media, journalists and responsible editors. Nevertheless, the way in which conflict resolution and peace processes are reported calls for fundamental rethinking and a new ethical direction. Bias and distortions in reporting religion's potential for violence inevitably have a destructive influence on public and political opinion and can weaken or impede initiatives for peace. But the most difficult and demanding task in situations of conflict is how to overcome violence and contribute constructively to a just and lasting peace. Success in this could rightly be called sensational, and anyone, religious or secular, contributing to it would deserve full media and public recognition. In addition to informing and enlightening, the media would then have achieved something desperately needed in peace processes: *empowerment*.

References

Albrecht, Ulrich / Becker, Jörg (eds.) (2002), *Medien zwischen Krieg und Frieden*, Baden-Baden: Nomos-Verlag.

Appleby, R. Scott (2000), *The Ambivalence of the Sacred. Religion, Violence, and Reconciliation*, Lanham: Rowman & Littlefield.

Basedau, Matthias / Körner, Peter (2009), *Zur ambivalenten Rolle von Religion in afrikanischen Gewaltkonflikten (Forschung DSF no. 18)*, Osnabrück: DSF.

Czada, Roland / Held, Thomas / Weingardt, Markus (eds.) (2012), *Religions and World Peace. Religious Capacities for Conflict Resolution and Peacebuilding*, Baden-Baden: Nomos-Verlag.

Fischer, Sebastian / Gathmann, Florian (2010), Power-Protestantin schaltet auf Angriff, in: *Spiegel online 14.01.2010*, www.spiegel.de/politik/deutschland/ 0,1518,671728,00.html [retrieved 28.09.2010].

Hasenclever, Andreas (2003), Geteilte Werte – Gemeinsamer Frieden? Überlegungen zur zivilisierenden Kraft von Religionen und Glaubensgemeinschaften, in: Küng, Hans / Senghaas, Dieter (eds.), *Friedenspolitik. Ethische Grundlagen internationaler Beziehungen*, München: Piper, pp. 288–318.

Käßmann, Margot (2010), *Fantasie für den Frieden oder: Selig sind, die Frieden stiften*, Ffm: Hansisches Dr.- und Verl.-Haus.

Little, David (ed.) (2007), *Peacemakers in Action. Profiles of Religion in Conflict Resolution*, Cambridge / New York: Cambridge University Press.

Marsden, Lee / Savigny, Heather (eds.) (2009), *Media, Religion and Conflict*, Burlington: Ashgate Publishing Limited.

Sampson, Cynthia (1997), Religion and Peacebuilding, in: Zartman, I. William / Rasmussen, J. Lewis (eds), *Peacemaking in International Conflicts. Methods and Techniques*, Washington DC: U S Inst of Peace Pr, pp. 273–316.

Scherrer, Christian P. (1995), Der apokalyptische Völkermord in Rwanda und die Rolle der internationalen Gemeinschaft, in: Calließ, Jörg / Merkel, Christine M. (eds), *Peaceful Settlement of Conflicts. A Joint Task for International Organisations, Governments and Civil Society (Loccumer Protokolle 24/95, 2 vols), vol. 1*, Loccum: Evangelische Akademie Loccum, pp. 311–350.

Seiterich, Thomas (2010), Friede sei mit euch, in: *Publik-Forum* no. 13/2010, p. 21.

Weingardt, Markus (2010), *RELIGION MACHT FRIEDEN. Das Friedenspotenzial von Religionen in politischen Gewaltkonflikten*, Bonn: BpB (new edition BpB).

Weller, Christoph (2002), Friedensforschung zwischen Massenmedien und Krieg. Von der Manipulationsforschung zur konstruktivistischen Friedenstheorie, in: Albrecht, Ulrich / Becker, Jörg (eds.), *Medien zwischen Krieg und Frieden*, Baden-Baden: Nomos-Verlag, pp. 27–44.

Media and Religious Conflict: Experiences from Northern Ireland

Norman Richardson

Introduction

Northern Ireland – a tiny but notorious corner of north-western Europe – is a society attempting a journey beyond its recent civil conflict and violence. Despite a peace process that has been in place since the mid-1990s, it remains a divided society and is becoming increasingly diverse in ethnic, cultural and religious terms. Sectarianism continues to be a serious concern and there has been a significant rise in racist incidents over recent years. The task of developing inter-religious learning in Northern Ireland involves addressing issues of difference on all levels – relationships between Catholics and Protestants as well as between Christians and members of other religions and beliefs.

All institutions in Northern Ireland have had to find ways of responding to the region's long-term inter-community conflict. This has certainly been an issue for the religious communities, for education and also for the media in its various forms. All of these – religion, education and the media – are contentious areas and have, in fact, at some time been accused from various quarters of provoking or perpetuating conflict and also of failing to deal with it responsibly. At the same time it could be argued that these institutions have sometimes played a positive part in promoting mutual understanding and contributing to the process of building peace. This paper will explore some of the interfaces between religion, education and the media with the particular experience of Northern Ireland as its main focus.

The intercultural challenge

In the White Paper on Intercultural Dialogue issued by the Council of Europe in 2008, there is a statement on *Intercultural Competences* which effectively draws together these three areas:

"The competences necessary for intercultural dialogue are not automatically acquired: they need to be learned, practised and maintained throughout life. Public authorities, *education* professionals, civil-society organisations, *religious communities*, the *media* and all other providers of education – working in all institutional contexts and at all levels – can play a crucial role here in the pursuit of the aims and core values upheld by the Council of Europe and in furthering intercultural dialogue" (Council of Europe 2008, 4.3 – present author's italics).

There are many challenges for those who work in these fields. Can educators contribute positively to inter-religious understanding and help people to deal more effectively with human difference and cultural or religious diversity? Can the media support religious educators in the role of promoting and improving religious literacy? Are there any values that religions, educators and those who work in the media might share for the public good?

Before reflecting on the role of the media, however, it will be necessary to sketch out the religious and educational context within which these issues function in Northern Ireland, although in a brief paper it will be impossible to do justice to these themes.

Religion

Religion in Northern Ireland has often been viewed with deep suspicion by both religious and secular outside observers, as indicated in a 1977 Punch cartoon depicting lions in a Roman amphitheatre about to encounter a bunch of Christians: "Oh dear, not the *Irish* Christians again", they remark (cited in Elliott 2009, p. 1). Malachi O'Doherty, a Belfast-based religious affairs journalist, has described Northern Ireland as "the tetchiest religious environment in Europe" (O'Doherty 2003, p. 126). The common usage of the terms 'Protestant' and 'Catholic' to describe the conflicting communities leads many to perceive Northern Ireland in terms of an anachronistic religious war. Out of frustration with this oversimplistic analysis there has been a temptation by many to play down the role of religion and offer a more political and secular analysis. There is no doubt that conflict in Ireland is significantly about territory, identity, political and economic power and conflicting senses of history, to name but a few, but the religious factor cannot be ruled out of the equation. Despite growing secularisation and disenchantment with the Churches and organised Christianity many people still comfortably describe themselves as 'Catholic' or 'Protestant', whether or not they are active or even believing members of those communities. Various studies have demonstrated that the close links between the two dominant forms of Christianity with community identity, cultural Irishness or Britishness, political loyalties and national aspirations, go very deep (Mitchell 2006, pp. 59ff). Yet to describe the Northern Irish communities just as 'two traditions', with all the im-

74

plication of homogeneity, is again to over-simplify; internal diversity within the political and religious communities is no less significant than if we were attempting to describe any other religious tradition – as all good religious educators should know!

One of the undoubted characteristics of Christianity in Northern Ireland is the strength of religious conservatism. This is particularly evident within almost the whole range of Protestant denominations, where, despite considerable breadth and diversity, conservative evangelicalism is regarded by many as the normative position. Within evangelicalism the theologies of Biblical literalism and even an aggressive creationist fundamentalism tend to be very influential and sometimes rather intimidating. The Roman Catholic Church, which still attracts significant loyalty from many of its members if measured in terms of mass attendance and adherence to Catholic schooling, also appears generally conservative and traditionalist, if less prone to excessive extremes, though it is not immune from the charge of fundamentalism, especially from some of its ex-members (O'Doherty 2003, p. 6; p. 126).

Ecumenism in Ireland has largely functioned as a top-down phenomenon and has therefore had little or no impact on most ordinary church congregations. Many smaller Protestant denominations completely oppose ecumenism, dismissing it as 'a Roman plot', and there are major disagreements about relationships with the Catholic Church even in the larger and more 'mainstream' denominations. Many Catholics pay polite lip-service to ecumenism but actual practice often suggests unawareness or indifference. More genuine ecumenical encounter tends to be found at the fringes of the churches, often among those who have felt increasingly isolated from defensive denominational conservatism. The existence of ecumenical peace and reconciliation movements like the Corrymeela Community, or of some of the 'social-conscience' Alternative Church movements, offers clear evidence of this.

Anti-Catholicism remains a powerful force within both religious and secular Protestantism. Elliott (2009, pp. 79–92) has indicated its historical origins, and its contemporary impact can be seen on the gable walls of some neighbourhoods, in the pulpit rhetoric of fundamentalist preachers and in the only slightly more guarded statements of some politicians. Strong feelings of this kind, divergent national aspirations and significant social separation of the communities lead almost inevitably to sectarian attitudes and behaviour. Religion is certainly not the only factor, but it may often be the attitudinal cement that holds the rest together.

Irish Christianity has not been immune from the impacts of secularisation, however, even though the process has been slower than in many other parts of Europe. In recent years it has been significantly accelerated in the Irish Catholic community by a range of child abuse scandals. In the 2001 Census just over 14%

of people did not respond to the question on religion or indicated that they had no religion (NISRA 2001); it would be surprising if this figure were not significantly higher in the forthcoming 2011 Census. There is little doubt that a growing number of people in Northern Ireland regard themselves as 'religiously unattached'.

Religious communities other than Christian have traditionally been small in number, though since the paramilitary ceasefires these communities have increased in size and also in visibility. Many churchgoing Christians, and the public in general, remain substantially uninformed about the beliefs and values of members of other faiths; public attitudes range from genuine welcome and inclusion, through indifference and ignorance, to outright hostility, sometimes expressed in religious terms such as "false" or even "satanic" and increasingly often in the form of racist attacks (Richardson 2008; 2009). Christian teaching in Northern Ireland has not been very good at helping church members to understand and value "the other". Within and between religious communities there is a need, at the very least, for significantly increased local and global religious literacy.

Religion and Education

If one of the best-known factors about life in Northern Ireland is its divisions between Catholics and Protestants, then almost certainly the best known factor about education in Northern Ireland is its fairly rigid division between schools on exactly the same basis. Many people appear to be comfortable with this continuation of separate parallel systems of schooling, and despite the existence of a vigorous movement towards integrated schooling over the past 30 years, the majority of children and young people – around 90% of the total – still attend schools that represent their perceived religious and cultural communities.[1]

Many observers have challenged separate schooling, expressing the view that if children in a particular society are taught separately throughout their most formative years we should not be surprised to find that society manifesting sectarian suspicions, divisions and in some cases outright hatred of those who belong to a different and unfamiliar community. In defence of their support for separate schools, particularly within the leadership of the Catholic Church in Ireland, it is argued that educational separation is a symptom, not a cause of the division. In this author's view cause and symptom have become inextricably

---

[1] It is important to clarify that almost all schools in Northern Ireland, including the vast majority of Catholic schools, receive full state funding.

entwined! There have been many voluntary and statutory curricular and extra-curricular initiatives designed to offset or overcome this separateness over the past four decades and some excellent work has been done to encourage awareness and mutual respect among children and young people (see Richardson & Gallagher 2011), but many of those working in the educational community relations field are well aware of the limitations of what they can do when children remain largely separate in their schools and communities.

If schooling is separate, so, inevitably, is Religious Education (RE). A 'Core Syllabus', devised by representatives of four Christian denominations, offers little more than a conservative list of largely Christian content to schools (DENI 2006). World religions have only featured on the syllabus since 2007 and only for pupils aged 11 to 14. In effect the teaching of RE in Catholic schools is largely catechetical in nature and, at primary school level, focused on preparing Catholic children for the sacraments of first confession, first communion and confirmation. In the state controlled schools (culturally Protestant in ethos) RE is largely biblical, and there is significant evidence that many teachers in controlled primary schools give little or no time to it. Recent research has indicated that many minority religion and belief families (including other world religions, humanists and those who declare no belief) are extremely dissatisfied with the Religious Education situation in Northern Ireland (Mawhinney et al 2010). The opportunities for children of Protestant and Catholic backgrounds to learn about each other's beliefs and practices are also very limited, and it could be validly suggested that the possibility of a religiously literate population is significantly disadvantaged by the combination of educational separation and an official approach to RE that lacks depth, breadth and vision.

Media

By means of television, radio, newspapers and, increasingly, the internet, these issues are frequently in the public eye, both within Northern Ireland and beyond it. Most often it is the negatives and disasters that catch the most attention. With increasing speed and intensity the divisions and conflicts of Northern Ireland – no less than any other perceived 'trouble spot' – are given global publicity by the media.

Most people would probably agree that the key roles of the media are to entertain and to inform. The balance between those roles will depend in part on the perceived audience and in part on the nature of the particular medium – we may justifiably expect more information from a public service broadcaster or a 'serious' newspaper than from a commercial television channel or a 'red top' tabloid. But might there also be grounds for arguing that the informational role of the media could or should go further and be perceived as a form of education? Indeed, can at least some parts of the media, even in an intense context like that of Northern Ireland, make positive contributions towards improved general religious literacy? Of necessity this examination must be brief and selective, so it is focused on public service broadcasting in Northern Ireland, with particular reference to religious affairs. In order to gain fuller insights into these issues, informal discussions were carried out with two of Northern Ireland's best-known religious affairs journalists: *William Crawley* of the BBC and *Malachi O'Doherty*, a freelance writer and broadcaster.

An excellent survey of the dilemmas facing a public service broadcasting organisation – the BBC – was carried out in the 1980s by Rex Cathcart (1984), an educationist and historian based at Queens' University Belfast. His analysis and many of his observations still ring true, even though he was writing at a time when the Northern Ireland 'Troubles' were at their height. Within the UK as a whole the BBC in Northern Ireland had been regarded over many years with considerable unease as (in the words of Cathcart's title) "The Most Contrary Region". How should such an organisation reflect a divided society? Cathcart's survey shows that to ignore the divisions and to ban controversy, as in the BBC during the 1920s and 1930s, was simply an abdication of social responsibility. The BBC reported on riots but avoided attempts to analyse or explain what was happening. They were nevertheless criticised by the pro-British political establishment for not offering an 'official' explanation, and some unionist politicians called for government control of news broadcasts. But at a later stage, in the years before the outbreak of civil unrest and political violence, attempts by the BBC to emphasise positive similarities and agreements between unionists and nationalists in Northern Ireland was, in Cathcart's view, simplistic and provided a false confidence that failed to probe the deteriorating political situation. Despite continuing criticism from both sides, either for their sins of commission or of omission, the position ultimately taken by the BBC during the 30 years of the troubles was to reflect the divisions in all their ugliness and to try to make sense of them, though the concern remained – and remains still – that such reportage should make every effort not to inflame passions and make the situation worse. There was a keen awareness that locally based journalists reporting on the conflict in Northern Ireland often had to make their way home through barricades, paramilitary patrols and volatile local situations!

When it comes to the question of how to represent the diverse religious communities – those who are often described in shorthand terms as 'Protestants, Catholics and others' – there are also many sensitive issues which have brought the broadcasters into conflict with one or more communities and also with politicians. Local journalists can easily be identified as either Protestants or Catholics and thus in some quarters their reports are treated as uncritical representations of their perceived 'side'. Malachi O'Doherty, a shrewd local observer of the religious and political scene, has described vividly how on several occasions he was greeted with varying degrees of hostility by Protestants as "that *fenian*[2] journalist" and on other occasions, when covering specifically Catholic situations, was invited to set aside his microphone and take part! This is despite the fact that O'Doherty is very open about no longer following the Catholic faith in which he was raised.

An attempt during the Troubles by the government to stop officials labelling victims of the violence by the terms 'Protestant' and 'Catholic', presumably on the assumption that this might reduce the potential for revenge attacks, failed partly by the frustration of the general public who have an insatiable desire to know "*what* someone is" and partly because of the determination of journalists to subvert this and find other ways of identifying victims. In taking these kinds of actions are the news media simply collaborating with the stereotyping of communities, or are they just reflecting the thinking of most members of the public?

There is a long tradition in Northern Ireland of people with strong, conservative religious views making their opinions known to the media, though this does not seem to happen with the same intensity as in previous decades. The most regular correspondents of this kind have tended to be evangelical or fundamentalist Protestants; those with a more liberal perspective and agenda appear more muted or more reluctant to speak out, perhaps through caution about being confronted by those with a more extreme agenda. Letters to the newspapers often quote the Bible in absolutist terms; presenters of radio phone-in programmes learned at an early stage of the value of keeping a Bible on hand to check the many references that were made by callers. Some organisations have from time to time set out to keep a tally of the number of Protestants and Catholics interviewed or otherwise featured in programmes, usually to point out that there were far too many from "the other community", and thus 'proving' the BBC's bias against them! A fundamentalist website has regularly featured calls for the sacking of William Crawley as presenter of BBC Radio Ulster's main religious current affairs programme, "Sunday Sequence", by alleging his antagonism towards evangelical Protestants in general and themselves in particular[3].

---

2   A historical term but often used by loyalist-protestants in a derogatory manner.
3   See, for example *CALEB DELEGATION MEETS BBC Belfast – Wednesday 25th November 2009*, on the Caleb Foundation website: www.calebfoundation.org (accessed 25/09/2010)

O'Doherty has written about the letters received from evangelical Protestants telling him that his journalism is blasphemous and that his punishment will be in Hell (O'Doherty 2003, p. 155).

Yet the voices representing the extreme positions are not excluded from the airwaves in Northern Ireland. Some programme makers have tried to make sure that such voices *are* heard and that contentious issues are aired. It has been suggested that in so doing the intensity of strong feelings is reduced by the very fact of being challenged by interviewers or other contributors, and that this can significantly diminish the potential for subsequent on-street antagonism, though this is hard to prove. Crawley suggests that it is not a good idea to edit out the extremist voices and that public exposure, supported by a strong interview and listener or viewer response, really does *expose* the weaknesses of such positions by democratising the conversation. As evidence of this he cites his own radio interviews with the Holocaust-denier David Irving and with one of the leaders of a dissident Irish Republican movement.

There are, nevertheless, times when judgements have to be made and it still may be necessary to edit out parts of interviews in order to protect an individual, to avoid extreme embarrassment or to avoid the possibility of retribution. O'Doherty has described a number of such incidents – such as when he interviewed a woman on the street for a response just after a major bombing incident in which nine civilians died and she justified it as straightforward revenge. But he questions whether it would have been better to trust the public to see that "the woman's logic was stupid" (*ibid*, p. 151).

Crawley believes that the public service broadcaster, by not having to "sell a product", is able to deal with an issue openly, honestly and in depth yet without having to take a position or take sides. In a society where many people find it difficult to talk publicly about religion, especially to people who are not part of their own faith community, he suggests that this is a very important function. O'Doherty argues that such a process inevitably improves the quality of the public debate, because "out there" the debate is usually very bad! It gives a voice; it can give permission to think outside the box; it can encourage dialogue; perhaps it can even help to prise open previously closed minds. At its strongest this contrasts with some other, blander forms of religious affairs journalism – as in a newspaper *Churches Page*, for instance, or in a denominational weekly or monthly journal.

Beyond the public service broadcaster's impartiality, however, the internet appears to be adding a new level of engagement with a range of issues. Many journalists, including the two to whom I spoke, are engaging in a more relaxed form of discussion – and perhaps also the expression of personal preferences or opinions – through their blogs to which listeners and viewers are often recommended during broadcasts. But while this encourages public engagement with important issues, is there a danger of turning the role of the professional observer and questioner into just another would-be opinion-shaper?

O'Doherty clearly values religious affairs journalism because it provides an opportunity to go to the heart of what people find important (*ibid*, p. 6). It is, for him, "the journalism of everything, particularly the direction of change in Irish culture and politics" (*ibid*, p. 136). In his view, however, the media in general has not been good at representing the traumas of people in the Northern Ireland conflict, and "has often preferred triteness to raw feeling" (*ibid*, p. 150).

In terms of its presentation of faith communities outside the Christian family there has been a danger of neglect due to the local obsession with relations between Protestants and Catholics. There has been some attempt to be more inclusive in the range of communities featured, but Crawley is concerned that the media's coverage of Islam, for example, all too often focuses on extremes and terrorism rather than on ethics, family matters or the significant historical contributions by Muslim scholars to science and society. In relation to secular beliefs, however, in otherwise conservative Northern Ireland it is notable that non-religious have taken their place among contributors to the short morning religious reflection on BBC Radio Ulster, *Thought for the Day*, whereas a debate still rages about whether this should be permitted on the national UK channel, BBC Radio 4.

Media as religious educator?

At the start of this paper the question was raised as to whether the media had any possible role in contributing positively to religious understanding and general religious literacy, especially in a divided society like Northern Ireland. At one level this may seem an unpromising suggestion, as there is clearly a lack of religious awareness in some branches of the media that expresses itself in indifference or in naive and over-simplistic monosyllabic headlines. Concern about such limited journalistic awareness and understanding has led the UK Bible Society (2008) to produce a downloadable guide for journalists covering many Biblical and ecclesiastical topics.

At the most obvious level schools broadcasting presents opportunities for extended awareness and deepened understanding, and there have been some excellent attempts in Northern Ireland to tackle controversial historical, cultural and religious themes and topics for children of all ages. The take-up of such programmes, however, does not always seem to be great despite the quality of production.

Neither Crawley nor O'Doherty seemed comfortable with the description of the broadcasting media as performing a direct educational function; broadcasters in religious affairs are clearly not teachers. There is, nevertheless, an important learning process that can be enabled by good quality broadcasting based on public service standards and values.[4] To achieve this both agree that the journalist has to have some of the characteristics of the cynic and to be willing to ask awkward questions. Through airing issues and interrogating people who hold particular views, especially strong views, there develops a very important Socratic process.

As religious literacy continues to decline – including, according to a very recent report[5], among practising members of some religious communities – the media can, and often do, provide valuable assistance to those charged with the task of more formal religious education. If future teachers of religious education are to fulfil the competences expected of them – including the requirement that they develop 'a knowledge and understanding of ... the significant features of pupils' cultures, languages and faiths' (GTCNI 2005, p. 14) – we will have to help them find good sources for their own personal and professional understanding. One of the first pieces of advice that I offer to my own student teachers as they commence their journeys of preparation to teach RE is to develop both their specific subject knowledge and their general knowledge, and among the suggestions I offer as to how they might achieve this, is to become avid listeners and viewers of good quality religious broadcasting.

In any society where religious views and opinions are strong and can sometimes be used to attempt to end discussion rather than to open it up, the media at its best can be a valuable ally in the process of promoting improved religious literacy and intercultural dialogue.

References

Bible Society (2008), *The Bible Style Guide: A resource for journalists and broadcasters*. www.biblesociety.org.uk (accessed 29/09/2010)

Cathcart, Rex (1984), *The Most Contrary Region. The BBC in Northern Ireland 1924-1984*, Belfast, UK: Blackstaff Press.

---

4   As articulated, for instance, in the ethical Code of Conduct of the National Union of Journalists; see http://media.gn.apc.org/nujcode.html (accessed 25/09/2010).

5   *US Religious Knowledge Survey*, issued by the Pew Forum on Religion and Public Life (September 28, 2010): http://pewforum.org/Other-Beliefs-and-Practices/U-S-Religious-Knowledge-Survey.aspx (accessed 30/09/2010).

Council of Europe (2008), *White Paper on Intercultural Dialogue. Living Together as Equals in Dignity*, Strasbourg: Council of Europe Publishing.

DENI (2007), *Revised Core Syllabus for Religious Education*, Bangor: Department of Education for Northern Ireland. http://www.deni.gov.uk/index/80-curriculum-and-assessment/80-curriculum-and-assessment-religiouseducationcoresyllabus-pg.htm (accessed 29/09/2010)

Elliott, Marianne (2009), *When God Took Sides. Religion and Identity in Ireland*, Oxford: University Press.

GTCNI (2005), *Teaching – the Reflective Profession*, Belfast, UK: General Teaching Council for Northern Ireland.

Mawhinney, Alison/Niens, Ulrike/Richardson, Norman/Chiba, Yuko (2010), *Opting Out of Religious Education. The Views of Young People from Minority Belief Backgrounds*, Belfast, UK: School of Law & School of Education, Queen's University Belfast.

Mitchell, Claire (2006), *Religion, Identity and Politics in Northern Ireland – Boundaries of Belonging and Belief*, Aldershot, UK: Ashgate.

NISRA (2001), *Northern Ireland Census 2001 Key Statistics – Table KS07c*, Belfast: Northern Ireland Statistics and Research Agency. (accessed 26/09/2010) http://www.nisranew.nisra.gov.uk/Census/Census2001Output/KeyStatistics/keystats.html

O'Doherty, Malachi (2003), *I Was a Teenage Catholic*, Cork, Ireland: Marino Books/Mercier Press.

Richardson, Norman (2008), Education for Religious Tolerance. The Impossible Dream? in: Patalon, M. (ed.), *Tolerance and Education*, Studia Kulturowa 2/2008: 39-53, Pedagogical Institute, University of Gdansk, Poland. http://studia.kulturowe.ug.gda.pl/sk-2.pdf (accessed 28/08/2009)

Richardson, Norman (2009), The Challenge of the New Religion and Citizenship in a Traditional and Conflicted Society. A Case-Study of Northern Ireland, in: Lähnemann, Johannes/Schreiner, Peter (eds.), *Interreligious and Values Education in Europe*, Münster, Germany: Comenius-Institut.

Richardson, Norman/Gallagher, Tony (eds.) (2011), *Education for Diversity and Mutual Understanding. The Experience of Northern Ireland*, Oxford, UK: Peter Lang.

Acknowledgement

I would like to express my appreciation to William Crawley and Malachi O'Doherty for their willingness to agree to informal discussion with me as I prepared this paper. Any interpretation of their views, however, is that of this author alone.

SECTION 2:
Theological, ethical,
and educational perspectives

The Ban on Images in a Media Culture Context. A Jewish Perspective

Jonathan Magonet

There are two aspects to this title, the Biblical prohibition on images and the so-called 'media culture', each of which requires separate treatment before attempting to bring them together. The use of the terms 'media culture' and especially 'media power' suggests that this is a new phenomenon or, at least, that in some ways it is new in terms of the power of the media to influence society. However the term 'media' represents a highly complex series of interconnected systems that play an enormous role in our society. They are the subject of any number of different kinds of research, study and evaluation. Moreover, the 'media', perceived as some kind of anonymous, omnipresent force, are often a convenient target for criticism and scapegoating when people feel that wrong values or information are being disseminated. Since media studies are not my personal field I am aware that my views are coloured by my own biases and prejudices. However these, in turn, are largely a product of whatever is currently fashionable, which is itself largely the product of the influence of the media. So, as a mere consumer, I want to acknowledge from the beginning my own limitations in addressing this topic.

Media in the Hebrew Bible

Insofar as the term 'media' describes different aspects of the communication of ideas or information to the widest public, some kind of communication system is a natural, and indeed essential, part of any organized society. Even the Hebrew Bible reflects both the use and abuse of the media by those who have the power to control it, and hence the need to scrutinize or combat their messages in particular circumstances. For example, the struggle to counteract state propaganda (or what today we might consider as 'disinformation') is a theme to be found in the writings of the Biblical prophets. In particular the prophet Isaiah satirizes the language and activities of the elite groupings of his society, the priests, prophets, politicians and military leaders, the wealthy and the sages (for example in Isaiah 5:8-23, 3:6-7). In one case he parodies an official government news release, which justifies a new political alliance as a protection against a possible invasion, probably by the Assyrian Empire. Isaiah substitutes the words 'death' and the 'netherworld' for the names of some known alliance partner, and the words 'lies' and 'falsehood' for the reassurance promised by the regime:

> Because you say, 'We have made a covenant with death, and with the netherworld we have made a pact; when the overwhelming scourge passes, it will not reach us; for we have made lies our refuge, and in falsehood we have found a hiding place.' (Isaiah 28:14-15)

Similarly, Jeremiah condemns the complacency of his contemporaries and their populist slogans about the invulnerability of Jerusalem because of the presence within it of the Temple:

> Do not trust in these deceptive words: 'this is the Temple of God, the Temple of God, the Temple of God'. (Jeremiah 7:4)

The banner headlines or billboards that we use today to attract attention or define opinions and attitudes have their Biblical counterpart. Habakuk is instructed:

> Then God answered me and said: 'Write down the vision clearly upon the tablets, so that one running past can read it.' (Habakuk 2:2)

Even the use of popular tunes with repetitive words to sell a message can be found, though in the case of the prophet Ezekiel it seems that his technique back-fires:

> As for you, son of man, your countrymen are talking about you along the walls and in the doorways of houses. They say to one another, 'Come and hear the latest word that comes from God.' My people come to you as people always do; they sit down before you and hear your words, but they will not obey them, for lies are on their lips and their desires are fixed on dishonest gain. For them you are only a ballad singer, with a pleasant voice and a clever touch. They listen to your words, but they will not obey them. But when it comes – and it is surely coming! – they shall know that there was a prophet among them. (Ezekiel 33:30-33)

And if the cult of the celebrity seems to be the overwhelming feature of contemporary life, this too must have had its Biblical counterpart:

> At the approach of Saul and David (on David's return after slaying the Philistines), women came out from each of the cities of Israel to meet King Saul, singing and dancing, with tambourines, joyful songs, and sistrums. The women played and sang: 'Saul has slain his thousands, and David his ten thousands.' (I Samuel 18:6-7)

One wonders who composed the song and how it was disseminated to 'all the cities of Israel'. Was it simply a spontaneous outpouring of joy and admiration, or, reading between the lines, the first step in a planned campaign on behalf of or by David, to gain power? Certainly Saul understood it that way:

> Saul became very angry and this matter was bad in his eyes for he said: 'They have attributed ten thousands to David but to me only thousands. All that he lacks is the kingship!' (I Samuel 18:8)

All the above examples are also reminders of the enormous power attributed to the word in the world of the Hebrew Bible, whether spoken or written. The Hebrew Bible begins with the creative word of God that brought into being the cosmos. The Hebrew *'davar'* means both word and 'thing'; a word is an event, an act that changes reality. The word can be used or abused since it is the source of knowledge, power, and authority. Blessings and curses have power to affect the recipient, and self-curses are carefully avoided or euphemized because of the harm they could do to the speaker if fully expressed. If our time is different it lies in the diminution of the power of the word because of the sheer volume of words with which we are daily bombarded.

There is an intermediate state between the word itself and the graven image which is prohibited in the Ten Commandments. This is the use of physical symbols and symbolic actions to express ideas and communicate a message. The prophet Jeremiah walked the streets of Jerusalem carrying a wooden yoke on his shoulders to symbolize that the nation would come under the yoke of the King of Babylon. He was challenged to a public debate by Hananiah, who also bore the formal title of 'prophet', and who seems to have represented the official government line. Hananiah dramatically took the yoke from off Jeremiah's shoulders and smashed it, claiming to speak in God's name: 'Thus will I break off the yoke of Nebuchadnezzar, King of Babylon.'. In the moment Jeremiah received no word from God, and he had to leave, apparently defeated, because he lacked a ready answer. In this classic media event, a precursor of presidential television debates, rhetoric won out over revelation, style and technique over truth. But, as the text indicates, though Hananiah seemingly won the public debate, appealing to the public need for reassurance, he lost the true word of God in that moment. (Jeremiah 28).

Graven Images and Idolatry

In the conventional Jewish numbering of the Ten Commandments, the prohibition on making a graven image is subsumed under the command to have no other gods, as the second commandment. (Exodus 20:3-5) Thus the essence of the prohibition is not the making of a tangible image itself but the purpose for which it is used. Moses himself, at God's command, made a bronze serpent that he displayed as a way of curing snakebites (Numbers 21:6-9). It was only the reforming zeal of King Hezekiah that led to it being destroyed because people had come to use it for worship purposes. Moreover Moses commanded Bezalel to construct the various artifacts (Exodus 31:1-11) that were to furnish the tabernacle, including the golden cherubim (Exodus 37:7-8). As the episode with the golden calf indicates, the central concern in this Commandment may not be the manufacture of a graven image itself. Rather the real issue is expressed in the continuation of the passage: 'you shall not bow down to them nor serve them'. The danger they represent is that they might be used as 'other gods' in place of, or alongside, or even as representations of Israel's God.

Furthermore, the text also specifies that these graven images should not represent anything that is 'in the heavens above or on the earth beneath or in the waters beneath the earth', presumably reflecting the range of images used for worship in the surrounding contemporary world. However, within the Exodus version of the Ten Commandments the Shabbat is designated as God's day of rest having created these same three domains and all that inhabits them, 'the heavens, the earth and the sea and all that is in them'. So to worship any one of these creations of God is to demean the power and authority of their Creator.

The distinction between the making of graven images and their use for idolatrous purposes finds its expression within rabbinic tradition. Already the Mishnah addresses the issue in the story of Rabban Gamaliel who bathed in the Bath of Aphrodite in Acre.

> *Proklos the son of Philosophos asked Rabban Gamaliel in Acre while he was bathing in the Bath of Aphrodite, saying to him, 'It is written in your Torah, "nothing of the banned thing (idol) shall cleave to your hand." (Deut 13:18) Why then do you bathe in the Bath of Aphrodite?'.... He answered, 'I did not come within her boundaries; she came within mine! They do not say, "Let us make a bath for Aphrodite", but "let us make an Aphrodite as an adornment for the bath". Moreover, even if they would give you a lot of money you would not enter before your goddess naked, or after a seminal emission, nor would you pass water before her! Yet this goddess stands at the mouth of the gutter and all people pass water before her. It is written: "Their gods" (Deut 12:3) only; so what is treated as a god is forbidden, but what is not treated as a god is permitted.' (Mishnah Avodah Zarah 3:4)*

Once this separation, between the graven image and its idolatrous purpose, has been made, the issue of reproducing images ceases to be a major concern. Or better expressed in terms of Jewish history, the use or prohibition of images is largely determined by the culture within which Jews have lived. In Christian Europe Jews produced illuminated manuscripts using human figures or, as in the case of the so-called Bird's Head Haggadah, human figures with their heads replaced by those of a bird, thus creating non-natural forms. In Islamic society the stricter ban on imagery affected Jewish artistic works and calligraphy was emphasized.

But uncoupling imagery from idolatry does not remove the essential issue of the nature of idolatry itself. The Hebrew text of the opening of the second commandment contains a number of challenging problems. Literally it reads: 'There shall not be to you other gods upon My face', the closing phrase being understood variously as 'in My presence' or 'besides Me'. But however understood the essence of the prohibition is the replacement in any way of God with another object of worship. This applies literally to the practice of various religious communities of the Biblical period that worship physical representations of their gods. Psalm 115 attacks those who create idols: 'they have eyes but do not see, ears but do not hear, ...' which the Psalmist defines as 'the works of human hands' (Psalm 115:4). The worship of such artifacts is essentially the worship of one's own human creations, that is, of oneself. Hence the opening phrase of the Psalm, 'not to us, O Lord, not to us, but to Your name give glory' (Psalm 115:1). The same idea is expressed by Hosea:

> *That we no longer say 'our god' to the works of our hands (Hosea 14:4).*

Once this identification has been made other objects of 'worship' can be identified, in a move from the literal to the metaphorical level. Job seemingly separates the 'gold', with which idols are overlaid, from its decorative purpose, and recognizes the celebration of wealth itself as an idolatrous act.

> *If I have made gold my trust, or called fine gold my confidence; if I have rejoiced because my wealth was great or because my hand had acquired much; if I have looked at the sunlight when it shone, or the moon moving in splendour, and my heart has been secretly enticed, and my mouth has kissed my hand; this also would be an iniquity to be punished by the judges, for I would have been false to God above. (Job 31:24-28)*

Jeremiah suggests other human attributes that can come to be regarded as ends in themselves, and thus substitutes for God:

> *Let not the wise man glory in his wisdom; let not the strong man glory in his strength; let not the rich man glory in his riches. But only in this should one glory, that one knows and understands Me. (Jeremiah 9:22-23).*

Leon Roth, summarizing the writings of the great mediaeval Jewish philosopher Maimonides, defines idolatry along these lines: "Idolatry has many forms but it is primarily the worship of the created, not the creator; and the human behaviour consequent on it is the egocentric going astray after the desires of man's own heart and eyes." (Roth 1960, p. 181)

In her commentary on the Book of Exodus, Nehama Leibowitz quotes the twentieth century Jewish philosopher Franz Rosenzweig on the nature of contemporary idolatry:

> "Names change but polytheism continues. Culture, civilization, people, state, nation, race, art, science, economy and class – here you have what is certainly an abbreviated and incomplete list of the pantheon of our contemporary gods. Who will deny their existence? No 'idolator' has ever worshipped his idols with greater devotion and faith than that displayed by modern man towards his gods ... a continual battle has been going on to this very day in the mind of

man between the worship of the One and the many. Its outcome is never certain." (Leibowitz 1976, p. 321)

The Psychoanalyst Erich Fromm addresses the underlying nature of this form of idolatry: "The history of mankind up to the present time is primarily the history of idol worship, from the primitive idols of clay and wood to the modern idols of the state, the leader, production and consumption – sanctified by the blessing of an idolized God.

"Man transfers his own passions and qualities to the idol. The more he impoverishes himself, the greater and stronger becomes the idol. The idol is the alienated form of man's experience of himself. In worshipping the idol, man worships himself. But this self is a partial, limited aspect of man: his intelligence, his physical strength, power, fame and so on. By identifying himself with a partial aspect of himself, man limits himself to this aspect; he loses his totality as a human being and ceases to grow. He is dependent on the idol, since only in submission to the idol does he find the shadow, although not the substance, of himself." (Fromm 1966, pp. 36–37)

The playwright Arthur Miller adds a further dimension: "An idol tells people exactly what to believe, God presents them with choices they have to make for themselves. The difference is far from insignificant; before the idol men remain dependent children, before God they are burdened and at the same time liberated to participate in the decisions of endless creation."[1]

Does this description have any relevance in questions about the nature or significance of the media today? Certainly because of the ability the media have to determine popular attitudes and beliefs in today's society they sometimes seem to take on god-like power. It can be argued that the need of the media to promote sensationalism and feed an endless desire for titillation, with the object of increasing an audience, and hence revenue, leads to a distorted view of society. There is even a kind of vicious circle whereby, for example, the sensationalist reporting of terrorism leads to a consequent creation of a culture of fear and the attendant risk of scapegoating particular populations. This, in turn, feeds the terrorist activity itself because of the need for atrocities with more and greater impact so as to maintain recognition of a particular cause.

Conversely, it is a truism that good news is never reported, precisely because it does not excite or attract attention on the scale that bad news does. A small byproduct of this situation is the problem it poses to religious communities. Insofar as they wish to make their particular values known they are faced with the dilemma that the 'good deeds' which are an essential part of their purpose are simply not 'newsworthy'. Thus they have to find ways of playing the media 'game'

---

1   From *Timebends: A Life* quoted in *Forms of Prayer*, p. 32.

if they do wish to promote themselves. But this has a number of inherent dangers. A pithy expression sums up the task of the advertiser in promoting a particular product: 'don't sell the sausage, sell the sizzle'![2] Yet precisely 'selling the sizzle', finding or inventing some kind of newsworthy feature, carries with it the serious risk of actually distorting the religious message itself because of the means that have to be employed. As Rabbi Lionel Blue once expressed it: 'The task of religion is to make the world more religious, but the danger is always that instead the religion simply becomes more worldly.' This is one example of the interface where our values are challenged precisely because of the seductive power of the media gods.

But with all these reservations about the power and influence of the media, there are important new realities that need to be acknowledged. At least in Western democracies, there are no secrets anymore. Hence, the failings of religions themselves can now be exposed and serious wrongdoing can get a public examination and, where appropriate, condemnation. Insofar as 'justice' is a significant part of any religious system this openness to scrutiny can only be welcomed. However, once again this is a two-edged sword. For the courtroom of the media is not the dispassionate and fair courtroom that, at least in theory, is to be found in a proper system of justice. Reputations may be destroyed without recourse to appropriate deliberation and judgment, and a public misperception of an individual or institution can never be completely corrected. This problem actually leads us back to the Ten Commandments, but not to the graven images of our title.

Bearing False Witness

The Ninth Commandment, 'You shall not bear false witness against your neighbour', within its Biblical context, seems to be related to court proceedings and the supplying of false evidence that creates problems and possibly serious dangers for your neighbour. Jewish tradition explores the broader issue of any kind of talking about one's neighbour by including two other Biblical prohibitions, the categories of *'rechilut'*, tale-bearing and *'lashon ha-ra'*, (literally, 'evil tongue') gossip. Maimonides sums up the implications in his Code of Jewish Law:

> *Who is a talebearer? One who carries gossip, going about from person to person and telling: 'So-and-so said this; I have heard so-and-so about so-and-so.' Even though he tells the truth, he ruins the world. There is a still worse iniquity that comes within this prohibition, namely:*

2   I am grateful to Jenny Pizer for this phrase. For non-English speakers, the 'sizzle' is the sound of the sausage cooking in the frying pan!

the evil tongue of the scandal-monger who speaks disparagingly of his fellow man, even if he tells the truth. (Code, De'ot 7:2)

Yet 'tale-bearing' and 'gossip' are the bread and butter of the media. The trivia of the lives of so-called celebrities become heralded as ultimate truths for daily consumption. Yet there is also a vicious undercurrent to the promotion of such people in the simultaneous attempt both to deify them and then destroy them should they display their common human flaws. And because these matters take centre stage in the headlines and degree of coverage, the real struggles, conflicts and suffering to be found around the world may be sidelined, or, worse, are also only real for us if reported. Tragically, they too are subject to fashion, and when interest fades they disappear from the public gaze to be replaced by some new sensation. Father Gordian Marshall once defined 'fundamentalism' as 'selective literalism'. By that definition we could include the mass media as today's ultimate fundamentalism, selective in what they choose to report and often simplistic in how they report it. But then we have to acknowledge that the media only give us what we wish to see and hear. They are not independent of our values, rather they reflect back to us precisely the values which we hold. Therein lies the disturbing truth of this contemporary form of idolatry, this particular kind of self-worship.

The media are a given of our contemporary culture. At the very least, as religiously oriented people, we should encourage a 'hermeneutics of suspicion' when experiencing their influence. So I want to conclude with a story that I have often told because of its personal impact on my own reading of the Bible. In 1968 I participated in an international Jewish youth conference in Edinburgh. In attendance were a number of Jewish students from Czechoslovakia. They stayed on for the Edinburgh Festival but during that time the Russians invaded, turning them overnight into refugees. But the story goes back to the conference itself where we studied some Biblical texts together. I was impressed with their reading skills, particularly as they had never studied the Bible before. When I asked them how this was, they explained: when you read a newspaper in Czechoslovakia, first you read what is there. Then you ask yourself, if that is what they have written, what really happened? Then you ask, if that is what really happened, what are they trying to make us think by what they have written? And if that is what they are trying to make us think, what should we think instead? We learn to read between the lines of the newspaper as if our life depended on understanding it!

The media are not necessarily the agencies of a suppressive state, and their practitioners may themselves be torn between their personal values and the particular interest, political or commercial, that they are employed to promote.

However, a healthy scepticism about the ideas and opinions with which we are daily presented seems to be an essential survival strategy. And since, unlike the idols of the Psalmist, we do have eyes with which to see, we should forever be on the lookout for the seductive forms of idolatry that we ourselves are forever inventing and re-inventing.

References

Assembly of Rabbis (ed.) (1995), *Forms of Prayer. Pilgrim Festivals*, London: Reform Synagogues of Great Britain.

Fromm, Erich (1966), *You shall Be As Gods. A Radical Interpretation of the Old Testament and its Tradition,* New York: Holt, Rinehart and Winston.

Leibowitz, Nehama (1976), *Studies in Shemot. The Book of Exodus,* Part I (Tr Aryeh Newman), Jerusalem: World Zionist Organization.

Roth, Leon (1960), *Judaism. A Portrait*, London: Faber and Faber.

Pictures and Symbols: An Islamic Perspective

Saeid Edalatnejad

The production and use of representational arts depicting living creatures are regarded forbidden in the Islamic traditions and judicial rulings. Such manifestations of art include painting, drawing, sketching, engraving, photography, and sculpture. In spite of this viewpoint among jurists, one can find some degrees of the development of those arts, especially in the modern time, in Muslim countries. The main question raised here is why those arts were forbidden in early and middle centuries of the Islamic history, and then on what grounds the application of those arts in the modern time can be justified. The present paper focuses on Shiite Islamic viewpoint and especially on the Iranian community, seeking to explain firstly the justification of the prohibition offered by jurists and then to analyze some critiques and terms applied in legal sources concerning the issue. Through analyzing, the paper intends to explain the reason of the production of those manifestations of art, especially the art of cinema, and refers to the main theoretical difficulties which Iranian artists have encountered in displaying their artifacts. It is worth mentioning that in spite of jurists' viewpoints the use of pictures and different symbols in poems and mystic teachings has been common but this paper does not take this aspect of application into consideration.

The main argument of jurists refers to those sayings attributed to the Prophet Muhammad and to the Shiite Infallible Imams, especially to the sixth Imam, Ja'far b. Muhammad al-Sādiq (d.148/765). To justify the theoretical foundations of prevention, it is pertinent to analyze the context in which those sayings were formed. The act of worshiping a variety of idols that represented different whims and infatuations of people was common in pre-Islamic Arabian community which referred to as *al-Jahiliyya* period when people believed that those sculptures and idols might make intermediaries between them and God. The belief was probably like that of theory of ideas and the role of gods in the philosophy of Plato. According to Islamic sources, those people gradually came to forget that intermediate role and regarded them as gods. There are evidences in the Quran that indicate the assumption that the main aim of the Prophet Muhammad was to disseminate the Islamic monotheistic cosmology amongst those people at the expense of disregarding the role of the idols and gods. One of the noticeable genres that may be regarded as the best evidence is expressed in the form of the genre of the histories of other pre-Islamic prophets in the Quran. In this genre, the history is regarded history as account and is being quoted according to the main aim of the Quran, not to what really happened. Thus, it is pictured as if all prophets had a common purpose for their people: preventing them from worshiping gods, hence guiding them towards the monotheistic cosmology. For example, the Quran (21: 52-57, 67) reads the sentence of Ibrahim to the audience, "What are these images to which you are so devoted?" and then his people said: "We found our forefathers worshiped them". "You and your forefathers have been in such obvious error", Ibrahim remarked in return. Conforming to the way of Ibrahim, the Quran quotes his key statements, "By God, I am planning to confound your idols once you have turned back..., shame on you and on whatever you worship instead of God, don't you use your reason".

Given the main teaching of the Prophet Muhammad was to proclaim monotheistic cosmology, it was necessary to prevent people from returning in any way towards remembering those idols. It is assumed that by painting, engraving and making sculpture, it would be probable that people may come back, or at least intend, to their previous tenets. In addition, the images among different people, especially in Arabia, had not any function, save being worshiped and making intermediaries between people and God. The artistic-cum-symbolic aspects of images and sculptures were not considered at all or, in a better word, never were known. According to Ibn Khaldūn[1] (d. 784/1382), the Muslim historian sociologist and philosopher, the Arabs became familiar with arts and techniques after their conquests because they were achievements of civilization and urban life, a phenomenon that Arabs had not already seen.

More evidence for confirming the assumption that people may return to pre-Islamic period through seeing the images is available in the traditions attributed to the Prophet Muhammad and to the sixth Shiite Imam, Ja'far b. Muhammad al-Sādiq. In one of their quotations, the act of making images is regarded absolutely as a kind of pseudo-divine creation that it is expected to breathe out by the maker on the Day of Judgment in order to become living creatures. Since the maker cannot do that, s/he should avoid making them here or, upon doing so, s/he is expected to bear the punishment in the Hereafter (al-Hurr al-'Āmilī, d. 1104/1693, (ed.) 1992, vol. 12: 220; al- Ansārī, d. 1281/1864, 1994, vol. 1: 184). Any attempt to restore the memoirs of the pre-Islamic period is regarded as "strictly forbidden" in those sayings. Two forbidden acts in some traditions (al-Ansārī, *ibid*: 184-185) are paralleled and caused to be non-Muslim, who may commit them: restoration of forefathers' tombs and making images. Both regarded as instances of the reverence to the tenets of pre-Islamic period. In an-

---

1   See concerning his life, "Ibn Khaldūn" in *Encyclopaedia of Islam*, second version, by M. Talbi. Leiden: Brill, 1960-2004.

other tradition (Bukhārī, 1981, vol. 5: 15-16; al- al- Hurr al- 'Āmilī, vol. 5: 308) it is said that the angles do not enter any house wherein dogs, images of animals or men are kept. In the context in which any reminiscent of the pre-Islamic period should be forgotten, some traditions (al- Hurr al- 'Āmilī, vol. 5: 307) even forbade to entertain babes or children by dolls. Further, it is advised that a Muslim does not say the prayer in front of the images that reflect living creatures and, also, fires; this is because performing such prayer would be like worshiping them. Strong evidence in traditions gives more support for the assumption that it would be probable that people may return to their previous tenets through seeing images and sculptures, hence they are advised not to keep such images in their homes. Otherwise, it is better to cut off the head of the image or to blind one eyes of the image, whether a sculpture or painting of animals or men (see, al-Hurr al- 'Āmilī, *ibid*). It is assumed that the defective images are not reminiscent of previous tenets, nor can they be regarded as agents of making respect in the mind of who see those defective images.

Reading the verses of the Quran and traditions with a hermeneutic approach indicate that ancient theological atmosphere. Hence, it would not be surprising to find such tenets in the context. Nevertheless, it is surprising that when any image is regarded as a reminiscent of the pre-Islamic period, it became such a dominant atmosphere in the minds of Sunnite and Shiite jurists. Through interpreting the verses and traditions in a classic method and often verbatim, most jurists, accordingly, considered any representational arts as forbidden acts. There is no need to list chronologically here the name of the jurists from the earliest centuries down to the modern time who believed that a Muslim should keep away from those arts that represent living creatures.[2] There is no reason, as far as I researched in sources, for forbidding making images of the Prophet Muhammad and Imams save aforementioned argument; even though it may be found other interpretations in popular beliefs. That is why the art of making images and sculptures in Islamic culture have not any progress. Instead, the noblest visual art is the art of calligraphy and transcription of the Quran wherein the art applied is considered as a sacred mode of art. Calligraphy in the Islamic culture is like that of the art of making images or iconography in Christianity, for calligraphy represents visible body of God's word (see, Burckhardt, 1967: 135 ff.).

As a sign of encountering religion with modernity, in the second half of the 20th century, some Shiite jurist criticized the jurists' previous understanding concerning the traditions related to the prohibition of making images. The most important criticism was that the punishment promised in the traditions, as attributed

---

2   See, for example: Muhaqiq al- Hillī (d. 676/1277, 1988), vol. 2: 263; Allāma al- Hillī (d. 726/1325, 1991), vol. 5: 257; al- Shahīd al- Awwal (d. 786/1384, 1990), 92.

to the Prophet and Imams, on making images, was not absolute, rather it was relative to those images reminiscent of the idols and pre-Islamic tenets and acts. The content of the traditions also refers to those images which, in the view of their maker, are intermediary between God and man. It is said that the belief in the idols and the possibility of directing people to worshiping them no longer exists in Islamic countries and, as a result, the prevention of practicing representational arts for that reason does not make any sense today. One of those jurists was Ayatollah Khomeini (1989, vol.1: 169-171) who believed that the prohibition of making images in Shiite traditions is related only to those that of the picture or the image which remind the pre-Islamic period, such as those refer to Zoroastrian images that remain from the majesty period of ancient Iran. Similarly, he (*ibid*: 172, 177-179) believed that those traditions firstly do not point to absolute sculptures but only to that of representing living creatures; secondly, they refer to those sculptures which in the belief of the maker betoken gods. According to him, if the maker of dolls and sculptures is a machine and the role of man in the process of making is limited to turning on the machine, those narrations do not indicate prohibition of the process of making such products. This is because nobody expect from the machine to breathe out and to create living creatures. On the basis of this argument, he permitted production and use of different images and movies. In his view, the way of breathing out defined in traditions attributed to the Prophet indicated on creating the man by the Hand of God is important for Him. He understood the narrations in a way that the prohibition of making sculptures had to do with referring to living objective creatures. Therefore, if someone assumes subjective images, e.g., angels and jinn, and then makes images of them, it will not be regarded as a prohibited act, for the process of their creation by God is not clear for us to say that there is some similarity between the creation of God and man. Thus from this viewpoint the content of narrations become conditional not absolute, but on the other hand, the result of his argument make a generalization. The generalization is that the use of whole images representing the ideas of pre-Islamic period would be forbidden, whether they represent living creatures or not. Ayatollah Khomeini (*ibid*: 176) did not avoid accepting this demand. The prohibition in his view includes the act of agent as well as order.

However, the term "reminiscent of" in the argument is ambiguous and apparently means that kind of reminiscence associated with polytheistic tenets. This is because he himself (*ibid*: 177) stated that it is permissible if someone sells or purchases those images and sculptures as antique objects or as a souvenir. One can conclude, from the statements of jurists that there is no reason except a theological one in prohibition of making images in their viewpoint. An evidence for this conclusion is that the jurists permitted images and sculptures to be produced which are not usually installing but because they are used in objects such as carpets that one may put his leg on rather than giving her or his reverence to it (see as examples, al- Tusī, s. d., 403; al- Shahīd al- Thānī, 1989, vol. 3: 211; Al-lāmma Hillī, s. d., vol. 1: 588, vol. 2: 579). If there were another criterion in prohibition save the theological one, the permission would not make any sense. Even though, practically speaking, the use of images and production of sculptures of Muslim famous Muslim personalities after the 1979 Revolution are current, the criticism of Shiite jurists' opinion is not yet comprehensive.

The second reason for expressing opposition against representational dramatic arts in the Islamic culture is that jurists believe that those arts may imply some immoral scenes and consequences. Here the concept of "immoral" in their terms is an utterly vague term that receives a wide range of instances in different cultures. On the one hand, the extreme instance of being "immoral" may be pornographic images that all religions agree on regarding them immoral and, on the other hand, the instance may be a portrait of a female such that there may not be any consensus, even among Shiite jurists, on regarding it as an "immoral" image. The reason for the ambiguity of the concept "immoral" depends, at least in this example, on the content of Islamic sources and, consequently, on the jurists' view concerning females and their relationship with males. According to the early as well as recent Quran exegetes, the female is one of the properties of the male, whether be her father or husband, and any occupation in the property without permission of the owner is unlawful and illegal. The veil means putting a boundary or fence around the property of the male and the breakdown of this boundary is regarded an immoral act. Furthermore, it is pertinent to note that the whole body of a free Muslim female, except her face and back of her hands in some Islamic traditions, is interpreted as genital organs ('awra) which should be concealed (see as examples, al- Tusī, 1986, vol. 1: 393- 396; idem, 1978: 258; Al-lāmma Hillī, 1991, vol. 2: 98; al- Shahīd al- Awwal, s. d.: 139). Therefore, the portrait and symbols of an unveiled female is tantamount to the breakdown of that boundary of the male's possession and to displaying of her genital organs that are certainly immoral in the jurists' opinion. As observed in this interpretation, the definition of "immoral" may include instances utilized in representational and dramatic arts, while those instances in other cultures are not regarded as "immoral". Once instances of immoral acts are reduced to displaying unveiled or naked females, all the more so in their viewpoint any image, movie and symbol, represent and imply the sexual organs of females. However, in our time, there exist some jurists who hold the view that permits images and symbols of females to be made and to be published, provided that they are not seductive. The extension of instances for the term "immoral" supports the idea that this concept is of relative, not absolute, truth. Thus, while moral issues are almost always complicated and can be difficult to agree upon, at least for some Shiite jurists, value-statements are often speaker-relative, whether implicitly or explicitly.

What is offered here on the interpretation of veil in Islamic culture is a fundamentally orthodox interpretation and differs from what religious intellectuals and some jurists try to say concerning the rights of women. They criticize that fundamental view that regard women as a property of the male and hold that the female has equal dignity and personality like that of the male. The female is entitled to wear any kind of cloths, which are not commonly regarded immoral, and that any relationship between male and female should not be considered as necessarily sexual. Thus, if the images and movies of female are made that are not immoral in the sense noted here, leading to fornication relationship, what reason would have been offered for the prohibition of creating images? This group of intellectuals and jurists interpret the term "genital organs" metaphorically, not verbatim.

There has been usually one exception in the Iranian community for making use of images, symbols, and recently movies. According to some jurists, the representational as well as dramatic arts that are supposed to serve dissemination of Islamic teachings and doctrines are permissible; if such manifestations of art may not imply any corruption. According as this view, in the Safavid period, Sheikh al-Islam Muhammad Bāqir Majlisī (d. 1110/1698, 1983, vol. 76: 284) believed that the use of those images and sculptures are permissible, provided that they are not prepared for being worshiped and are not reminiscent of the pre-Islamic period, rather they may serve dissemination of the Islamic doctrines. Majlisī documented his idea by making a reference to a Quranic verse (34: 13) in which God ordered the people of the Prophet David to give their thanks to jinn for making some images and shrines with his Lord's permission. God, here, as Majlisī understood, not only blamed jinn for making images but also ordered the people to praise them because their act was in service of God. By this justification, ta'ziya, as an archetype of Iranian drama, (see, Chelkowski, 1979, esp. 7-15) and pardekhānī, story-telling by referring to the portrait which are painted on the scale included scenes reminiscent of the events of Karbala and displayed for audiences, were accepted and legalized at least since nineteen century. In spite of preventing people from drawing any images and symbols betokening the Prophet and the Infallible Imams, one could find in story-telling the portrait of the Imam and his companion; also one could find in this drama (ta'ziya) a man who plays the role of the third Infallible Imam al-Husayn (d. 61/680), who was engaged and martyred in a battle against the oppression of Yazīd, a disqualified claimant of the post of caliphate in lieu of the Prophet Muhammad. This drama could benefit from appropriate music and symbols, too. For the first time in the Qajar period, it was Mīrzā abū al- Qāsim Qummī (d. 1231/1815) who issued a precept or fatwa on the lawfulness of dramatizing *ta'ziya* simply because it serves dissemination of more Shiite doctrines for people. As Shiites were, in practice, less opposed than Sunnis to physical images, Persia may have been the first Muslim state to encourage some kinds of those arts officially. Since 1844, when the art of photography was introduced to the Iran community and a department of photography was established at Dār al- Funūn in Tehran about 1860, the problem of permission for photography was put on the table for Shiite Iranian jurists. Nāsir al- Dīn Shah and Muzaffar al-Din Shah were interested in taking photos and persuaded the rest to do so. Most conservative groups accepted the permission of photography, for in their opinion it does not making a new image but recording the shadow of images.

Permission for using representational and dramatic arts in order to disseminate and support Islamic doctrines is the main reason of application those arts in modern time. The permission serves to reconcile the Islamic religion and media. This time, media is handmaiden of religion, instead of philosophy. However, since Iranian jurists have had a prejudice to the those arts, regarding them as Western phenomena which have no function save entertainment, in the first step they resist against permission and, in the second step, they cautiously give their opinion on its application. For example, When representatives of the first Parliament in Iran (1906) came to ratify the law of the municipality, some of them asked their colleagues to avoid mentioning some words such as 'theater' and 'museum' in the Parliament in which they called it as 'sacred *majlis or parliament'*. Since they believed that the Western word 'theater' was not appropriate for the dignity of the Parliament and the latter, 'museum', in their opinion, did not have any benefit (see, Mīrzā Sālih (ed.) 2004: 140). Another example is that most Shiite jurists absolutely forbade the use of radio, television, and cinema in Pahlavi period, since in their viewpoint the media concerned require some corruption in the faith of believers. Nevertheless, after the Revolution 1979, permitting the use of media, Ayatollah Khomeini regarded them as 'a university', provided they serve to promulgate 'Islamic doctrines' as well as useful information and provided they consider 'moral values'.

Ayatollah Khomeini's idea may have received a socio-political interpretation that is beyond of the scope of the present study. However, his legal standpoint concerning using media in the service of religion continued after him. Consequently, Iranian artists encounter with two important problems in practice. These problems are resulting from the vagueness of two concepts: 'Islamic doctrines' and 'moral values'. As to the former, since there are different readings of Islam, the main problem is that if the media function by utilizing those arts to promulgate Islamic doctrines, then which reading(s) of Islam would be in perspective:

fundamental, liberal, or ideological reading of Islam. This is a decisive problem particularly when the media in Iran are considered rather exclusively under the control of the government with its interests in disseminating the official reading of Islam. As to the latter, the interpretation of 'moral values' is at issue. The more interpretation is global in contrast to the local values, the more media are successful to communicate and convey ethical ideas to more audiences. The local interpretation from the jurists concerning 'moral values' poses restrictions for producing images and moves. One jurist may regard showing the simple portrait of a woman wearing the veil as 'a breakdown of moral values', as most jurists before the 1979 Revolution used to have such a belief, yet another jurist may not have such narrow views on the subject. In today Iran, there is an agreement among jurists that showing the female's portrait in the recorded program of television is lawful, but it is immoral and not permissible that male and female artists have physical contacts, even in the form of shaking hands with one another. This opinion makes harder production of images and movies that reflect the real emotion of life to the audience. Assume how hard it would be for a producer to show in a piece of film the emotional relationship, for example, between a mother and her son, a father and his daughter, and a wife and her husband. The complexity in this field is not limited to these issues. Iranian artists, however, have created methods to show such scenes without committing immoral acts as interpreted by jurists in their works during last 30 years. Exposition of those created methods is beyond the scope of this paper, however. It is appropriate to note that such theoretical ambiguities and practical complexities emphasize the need for more explanations and efforts to apply media for introducing religious and ethical values in Iran.

References

(Initial definite (al) is ignored in alphabetization)

Al- Ansārī, Murtazā (1994) , *Kitāb al- Makāsib* [*The Book of Jobs*]. Qum, Iran (Bāqirī).

Burckhardt, Titus (1967) *Sacred Art in East and West, it Principles and Methods*, tr. by Lord Northourne. Bendfont, (Middle Sex).

Bukhārī, Muhammad b. Ismā'īl (1981), *Sahīh al- Bukhārī*. Turkey, Istanbul (al-'Āmira).

Chelkowski, Peter, J. (1979), *Ta'ziyeh: Ritual and Drama in Iran*. New York (New York University Press).

Al- Hillī, Muhaqiq (1988), *Sharāyi' al- Islām*. Iran, Tehran (Istiqlāl).

Al- Hillī Allāmma (1991), *Mukhtalaf al- Shī'a*. Iran, Qum (Nashr al- Islāmī).

(s. d.), *Tadhkira*. Iran, Qum (al- Razawiyya).

Al- Hurr al-'Āmilī, Muhammad b. Hassan, (ed.) (1992), *Wasā'il al- Shī'a, ilā Masā'īl al- Sharī'a*. Qum, Iran (Mu'assasa Āl al- Bayt).

Khomeini, Rawh Allah (1989), *al- Makāsib al- Muharrama* [*Forbidden Jobs*]. Iran, Qum (Ismā'īlīyān).

Majlisī, Muhammad Bāqir, (1983), *Bihār al- Anwār*. Lebanon, Beirut (al-Wafā).

Mīrzā Sālih, Gh. (ed.) (2004), *Mudhākirāt Majlis Awwal: 1324/1906-1326/ 1908*, Iran, Tehran (Māzyār).

Al- Shahīd al- Awwal, Muhammad b. Makkī (1990), *al- Lum'a*. Iran, Qum (Dār al- Fikr).

(no print), *al-Dhikrā*.

Al- Shahīd al- Thānī, Zayd b. Ali (1989), *Sharh al- Lum'a*. Iran, Qum (Dāwarī).

The Quran

Al- Tūsī, Muhammad Hassan (s. d.), *al- Nihāya fī al- Mujarrad, al- Fiqh wa al- Fatāwā*. Lebanon, Beirut (Dār al- Andulus).

(1986) *al- Khilāf*, ed. 'Alī Shahristānī. Iran, Qum (al- Nashr al- Islāmī).

(1978) *al- Iqtisād*. Iran, Tehran (Jāmi' Chihilsutūn).

Media ethics as part of a public theology
– a Protestant perspective

Johanna Haberer

1. Four perspectives on why theology engages with the media and with the ethical perspective of the media

1.1

Christianity is a media religion. It can be perceived as a community of understanding, interpretation and narrative coming from oral tradition and set down in written form through a process of content selection. Christianity is a missionary religion. It was spread by preaching and letters which, in the course of the historical process of selection through interpretation and evaluation, acquired canonical status. It made use of music and images in order to pass on biblical narratives and the message of salvation. It was expressed through images in a centuries-long struggle over how images affect people, what magic lies within them – in other words, the debate between the prohibition of images and the likeness of God. (Hörisch 2010, pp. 29–35)

In Christian worship preaching developed as a particular form of oral exposition centred on God speaking directly to the individual. The sacrament of the Eucharist, the *media salutis*, was the way of enabling the closeness to God and his grace to be experienced (ibid.)

From its beginnings, the religion of Christianity has concerned itself with the phenomenon of attention ("Aufmerksamkeit"). What conditions are a prerequisite in being attentive to God? What laws are required to gain the attention of the many for the welfare and salvation of others? "The media" is the most important Judeo-Christian answer to this.

1.2

At the heart of Christian dogmatics is the teaching of God in the form of the doctrine of the Trinity. God is the mystery of the world, God communicates with Himself, and he communicates with humankind in Christ through the Spirit in the eternal loving tension between omnipotence and impotence. The idea of the

Trinity invites reflection on communication as a primal characteristic of the divine, communication as a leitmotif of theology, communication across the whole history of humankind as a process of conversation in God, communication as a virtual process in a long tradition of reflecting on virtuality, on the synchronicity of presence and absence, on symbolic communication.

Christian theology contemplates God through the Bible in a process involving discourse and hermeneutics with the divine inspiration of communication, speaking, listening, showing, of God's struggle to gain the attention of human beings, of human beings' struggle to be attentive to God.

1.3

Corresponding to this Trinitarian perspective is the biblical and Christian image of human beings. The individual is open to God, open to the world, in his or her likeness to God, rational, malleable, open to temptation, but capable of being convinced of what is good by argument and example.

The debate about paying attention to what is good and, beyond that, to what is transcendent, begins with the individual.

Human beings are made for communication and learning, they are educated and educate themselves towards the right kind of attention.

The media play a significant role in Christianity in the education of the individual, which is why theology has, from earliest times, engaged with how the media impact on the salvation and justification of human beings. The theological concept of justification means that the individual continues to grow towards being a socially integrated personality united with God.

1.4

In the Bible we can perceive patterns of journalistic thinking. The Bible speaks of the synaesthetic perception of God, whereby the concepts of "hearing" and "seeing" are given equal importance (Utzschneider 2007, pp. 328ff.). In the Old Testament the concepts of seeing, hearing and remembering are broadly expressed by the key Hebrew word *yada* which is generally translated as "to know" but more precisely "to perceive, to be attentive".

The Bible is a collection of examples of attentiveness. It is about paying attention and about the question: "To whom or what does a person give attention, to what are the senses directed and how does God gain a person's attention? From the very beginning, the Judeo-Christian religion has created literary genres:

from legal texts, poetry, narrative, prophecy and parables to the characteristic form of the gospel. There are also early texts which take the form of criticism and censure of those in power. An example of censure is found in Jeremiah 36, or, for example, the sober account of King David (Heym 2002) and the critical attitude of the chroniclers, difficult to imagine in the region at the time, notably the discussion between David and Nathan: "You are the man" (2 Samuel 12.7). The social structures and strategies mirrored here remind us of today's debates on professionalism among media representatives, and of distance or proximity to power, which in the Old Testament is found in the distinction between prophets of salvation and prophets of doom.

The Old Testament sets out clear criteria for those in power: political power must be open to criticism. The ruler should be self-critical, fear God, hold office in stewardship and work towards Shalom as a process and a task for the powerful; that is to say, social equilibrium as a vision of a just society, of social order and public organisation in which attention is paid to the poor and the powerless are given a voice.

Moreover, the media may be regarded in biblical terms as the media memory of society, and the duplications and repetitions of biblical traditions as early examples of multiperspectivity; the four versions of the life of Jesus and the regular debate on reconciling the differences may be understood as an example of media debate.

2. The Reformation tradition and its view of the media as mediating immediacy and attention, or: the pattern recognition of mass media discourse

Under the heading of "Information technology in search of a media event" historian Johannes Burkardt notes how the innovation of printing influenced the ideas debate during the Reformation (Burkhardt 2002, pp. 17ff.). Religious media discourse was disseminated through tracts and pamphlets, not only impacting on the political culture of Europe but becoming identified with it (Mörike 1995), shaping to this day the mass media debate in its various genres: information, commentary, essay, satire.

For an ethics of the public, further conclusions can be drawn from examples from the Reformation about the use of modern media. The Reformation believed that salvation comes through the Holy Spirit, in the understanding of justification for and through the individual. For the Reformation salvation became personal and individual, and might come about through the medium of music, art, speaking and preaching, through hearing or reading Holy Scripture and through the power of argument and conviction.

So individualisation of media consumption can be identified as an issue in the Reformation just as it is today with the debate on the social impact of the internet. Printing was, after all, – like the internet today – the only new communication technology to be welcomed by the religious communities in Europe (Burkhardt, ibid.). Later developments in the media, including newspapers, cinema, radio and television, ushered in innovations in technology and were always accompanied by the cautionary, admonitory voice of the church which saw them as rivals in the competition for the interpretation of events.

As well as focussing the media message of salvation on the individual the Reformation also provided the model for the Protestant view of the individual, self-empowered to take part in media debate. Of the five senses Reformation theology used the receptive sense of "hearing" for God, with the ear as the most important organ, but it also ushered in the era of the written word. Consequently, those wishing to participate in religious and political debate had to acquire the appropriate cultural tools: self-empowerment, competence and literacy emerged as a pattern of the Protestant Reformation. Literacy has received a similar boost from the internet, inasmuch as written forms of communication, such as email, are still seen as part of digital media.

Another typical example from the Reformation is the emancipation from dogma and rules, the questioning of authority and responsibility for one's own salvation (Ganz/Lentes/Henkel 2004). Taking responsibility for one's personal growth includes participating in debate and saying goodbye to the "expert". Lay people were encouraged to become involved. The Leipzig Disputation between Dr. Luther and Dr. Eck, and other similar debates among experts, were immediately familiar in pamphlet form among Luther's followers and were disseminated, well beyond academic circles, to a "reforming" public. Independent printers and huge circulations played a large role in this, thus creating a public media economy.

The principle of personalisation was also present in the Reformation, and is still an important principle for newsworthiness in the modern media business. Making use of the new media technologies, the reformers played with great skill on Martin Luther's gift for media presentation, such as the early mythologising of the "nailing of the 95 theses", the burning of the papal bull, or the announcement of his appearance at Worms, in order to apply public pressure and challenge the authority of the Pope. A variety of media was employed for the purpose of emancipation from the dominant religious and political authorities. A culture of public dispute was also fostered, and was accompanied by cartoons and satirical verses, polemic and defamatory songs. In Rome at the beginning of the sixteenth century the Pope found himself in a storm of controversy that is difficult to imagine today. By comparison the Muhammad cartoons which caused such a furore a few years ago are positively mild.

3. Types of ethic – a Protestant perspective

In the Protestant context engagement in media activity was followed only later by media ethics discourse. Protestant debate on media ethics has always taken place in the light of practical experience; rather than being purely theory based, media-ethical debate has relied on both theory and practice. For this reason interventions by the Protestant church are another important strand.

From the time of August Hinderer, director of the German Press Agency and professor of press and journalism at the Humboldt University in Berlin, the Protestant church in Germany has seen itself as part of the media in the public sphere, not as competing with the secular public. In the early part of the twentieth century Hinderer had opened a new chapter in relations between the media and the churches, which had long opposed a general public sphere not controlled by them (Höckele 2001). The Protestant church now saw itself as a player in the general media marketplace, and after the Second World War as advocate for the freedom of the press, regarding journalism as a means to that freedom, a position that goes back to the Protestant media representative Robert Geisendörfer (Schulz 2002). The freedom of the media, its quasi-prophetic independence from outside influence, whether political or economic, was the credo of the church's reflection on the media, as it asked to what extent the media are the voice of the voiceless.

In the excellent recently published "Handbuch Medienethik" (Handbook of Media Ethics) (Schicha/Brosda 2010) Schicha classifies media ethics in different ethical types, relating these to ethical issues in the media. It is a very useful approach which allows one to ask, from a Protestant perspective, what this has to do with the Protestant church: how does the Protestant church see its involvement in this ethical typology? What is its contribution to the debate?

The principle of *deontological ethics* (Kant), which judges the rightness of an action, requires that the individual is bound voluntarily to an obligation, and this can be seen in the various institutions of self-regulation of the media. As a socially relevant group, the churches have helped to initiate and set up these bodies, taking an active part in, for example, the broadcasting council and the self-regulatory body of internet providers (Stapf 2006). To do this they have to rely on the media expertise of their delegated representatives as well as the social force of argument.

With regard to the protection of young people the churches have been particularly involved in the prevention of violence. Here the churches intervene on the basis of *utilitarian ethics*. These debates evaluate the consequences of an action and introduce the teleological perspective. The Protestant church's input in the debate is concerned with the common good, or, as it is often called, *public value*, projecting a vision of a society in which the media serve a common value and a public interest, finding the right balance between the interests of society, in which the media promote the well-being of all, focussing public attention on those to whom society pays little or no attention.

The churches also support all forms of *contract models* (cf. e.g. Rawls 1979) and process models for the development of ethical judgement. They participate in media policy-making and model codes of conduct, and support all contract models of self-commitment and self-regulation in the media. The Protestant church takes part in current debate on ethics and case-based discourse in the media through its own publication (epd medien, cf. www.epd.de), which, with its Roman Catholic equivalent, is the only media-ethical publication on the market.

A *systems-theoretical approach* is also found in articles by the churches on the media debate in Germany and Europe, articles on the professionalisation of media producers, the founding of journalism awards and of a Protestant school of journalism. Saying there ought to be freedom of the media requires systems which give a real experience of this freedom, and people who have, themselves, received high quality professional training.

The principle of self-empowerment and growth in competence formulated in the thinking of the Reformed church is essentially *constructivist ethics*. The individual's capacity for responsibility is strengthened through the contributions of education, scientific observation of perceptual behaviour and opportunities to develop reflective attentiveness. A number of religious education specialists are working in this field, one of whom is our Nuremberg colleague, Manfred Pirner (cf. Kirchenamt der Evangelischen Kirche Deutschlands / Sekretariat der Deutschen Bischofskonferenz 1997).

4. Ethics in the public sphere

A Protestant ethic of the public sphere ought to examine the concept of "attention". It has often been an underlying theme in philosophy and theology, and in recent years has surfaced in different forms in discussions on culture. In the theological context it was examined some years ago by Günther Thomas, a systematic theologian in Bielefeldt, in an initial study of the theme (Thomas 2004, pp. 89–104).

The theme of "attention" has attracted attention from various quarters in academic debate (Assmann/Assmann 2001). In 1998 the cultural philosopher Georg Franck wrote about the currency of attention in the modern media world (Franck 2007). From his observations, people had never collectively, or with such dedication, embraced the idea of public attention being a measure of an individual's importance as in today's richest and most highly civilised societies. The richer and more open a society, the more overtly does social ambition become a main aim in life. In an affluent society it is not carefree enjoyment but the desire to be noticed that becomes the main aim in life – and the dominant angst.

Franck believes that attention, even in the nature of a gratuity, is gradually displacing the currency of money and that this is most noticeable among the experts in attention-giving: the media. By finding out, and delivering, what the public wants, the provider is attentive to the consumer, and the consumer pays for this in the currency of attention. The units of account in this exchange are circulation figures and ratings. The appeal of the media for the provider is that the potential for gaining attention through their channels is far greater than via the street or public space. The thrill of their business idea is in attracting attention strategically, continuously and on a large scale, with predictable outlay and revenue. The valuable commodity represented by being featured in the media is celebrity. Celebrities, according to Franck (2007) are the millionaires of the attention currency. The other side to the culture of media attention-seeking is described by Leipzig philosopher and sociologist Christoph Türcke who considers that the media society suffers from a cultural ADHD syndrome. In a mood of cultural pessimism Türcke asks what is happening to a culture which allows its dreams to be out-sourced to the media. The remedy he prescribes for attention deficit is to take time out for quiet reflection, or, in the words of Walter Benjamin, for "detention for the soul" (Türke 2009, p. 249).

Bernhard Waldenfels' fine book is a profound philosophical examination of the phenomenology of attention. In it he makes the case that human attention cannot simply be acquired. Attention occupies the space between the involuntary and voluntary act, between aesthetics and ethics, between what is and what ought to be. Although it is not possible to moralise about attention, there is always an ethical undertone: "We cannot remain indifferent to things that strike us" (Waldenfels 2005, p. 261). "Consideration is given to something or somebody, and beyond that esteem, which we either freely give or refuse, for attention always has a social connotation. Attention leads to consideration; consideration may become attentiveness, then regard and respect. The Dutch word for attention, incidentally, is aandacht...." (Ibid., pp. 261–269). [Translator's note: aandacht recalls the German word Andacht = prayer, meditation or worship].

The idea of attention spans what is involuntary and what is directed, what it is in practice and what it is as a market currency, and a Protestant public ethic has to grapple with this. Aleida Assmann distinguishes between strategic and transcendent attention, the one the result of presentation, the other describing religious wonder.[1] For a Protestant ethic this means that ethics are activities of perception, media ethics are training in modes of attention.

As the world of the media becomes ever more self-referential, observation is an important element of a Protestant ethic: observing and being aware of media structures and content as they develop. There is a creative tension between what is technologically possible and what society finds acceptable, between self-expression and alienation, between freedom and responsibility, between profit and the public interest. The church has to reflect on its own role as object or subject in media perception, on its role in canvassing for people's attention so that they turn their attention to God.

The second task concerns the language for describing new media phenomena. Protestant media ethics are all about language, describing and reflecting on media phenomena. Its method is through description; it opens up areas of language; it focuses attention on media phenomena other than law-breaking. For a Protestant media ethic the media are a cultural phenomenon whose processes have to be carefully examined.

From a Protestant perspective, attention follows a train of thought: how does media attention develop, and what ethical guide do journalists have when selecting items of news? Is there an ethic of newsworthiness? How can attention be focussed on those who are given none? How can the attention logic of a pure attention economy be interrupted (Galtung/Ruge 1965)? To what extent do the media serve the public interest? To what extent is theirs a responsible freedom? To what extent do they contribute to the maturity of the individual? What images do the media project of individuals and what is their attitude to the biblical view that human beings are in the likeness of God?

The Protestant concept of attention is casuistic: cultural and theological diagnosis is arrived at by applying reasoning to individual cases. To this end a Protestant media ethic creates attention for space for practitioners, observers and theorists to engage in authority-free debate on phenomena in the media; to enable alternative perspectives, self-reflection by media producers and, ultimately, greater quality. Finally, a Protestant media ethic attracts attention for interrupting

---

1   Cf. introduction by Aleida Assman in Assmann/Assmann, pp. 20ff.

the attention economy of the media, creating space for the "some extra time for the soul".

References

Assmann, Aleida / Assmann, Jan (eds.) (2001), *Aufmerksamkeiten*. [Conference of the working group "Archäologie der literarischen Kommunikation" October 1998, Vienna], München: Fink.

Burkhardt, Johannes (2002), *Das Reformationsjahrhundert. Deutsche Geschichte zwischen Medienrevolution und Institutionenbildung 1517 – 1617*, Stuttgart: Kohlhammer.

Franck, Georg (2007), *Ökonomie der Aufmerksamkeit. Ein Entwurf*, München: Dt. Taschenbuch-Verlag.

Galtung, Johan / Ruge, Mari Holmboe (1965), The Structure of Foreign News. The Presentation of the Congo, Cuba and Cyprus Crisis in Four Norwegian Newspapers, in: *Journal of Peace Research* 2, pp. 64–91.

Ganz, David / Lentes, Thomas / Henkel, Georg (eds.) (2004), *Ästhetik des Unsichtbaren. Bildtheorie und Bildgebrauch in der Vormoderne* [the papers in this volume were given at an international conference of the research group "Kulturgeschichte und Theologie des Bildes im Christentum" which took place from 7–10.12.2000 at the University of Münster], Berlin: Reimer.

Heym, Stefan (2002), *Der König-David-Bericht*, Frankfurt am Main: Fischer-Taschenbuch-Verl.

Höckele, Simone (2001), *August Hinderer. Weg und Wirken eines Pioniers evangelischer Publizistik*, Erlangen: Christliche-Publizistik-Verl.

Hörisch, Jochen (2010), Christentum ist Medienreligion, in: *epd medien*, No. 56/57, pp. 29–35.

Kirchenamt der Evangelischen Kirche Deutschlands / Sekretariat der Deutschen Bischofskonferenz (eds.) (1997), *Chancen und Risiken der Mediengesellschaft. Gemeinsame Erklärung der katholischen Deutschen Bischofskonferenz und des Rates der Evangelischen Kirche in Deutschland*. (Gem. Texte, 10), URL: www.alt.dbk.de/schriften/data/3587/index.html, last accessed 4.2.2011.

Mörike, Olaf (2001), Pamphlet und Propaganda. Kommunikation und technische Innovation in Westeuropa in der frühen Neuzeit, in: North, Michael (ed.), *Kommunikationsrevolutionen. Die neuen Medien des 16. und 19. Jahrhunderts* [Papers given at the 4th Salzau-Kolloquium on 2 and 3 May 1994 on the theme of "Kommunikationsrevolutionen im Vergleich"], Köln: Böhlau, pp. 15–32.

Rawls, John (1979), *Eine Theorie der Gerechtigkeit*. Berlin: Suhrkamp.

Schicha, Christian / Brosda, Carsten (eds.) (2010), *Handbuch Medienethik*, Wiesbaden: Verlag für Sozialwissenschaften.

Schulz, Otmar (2002), *Freiheit und Anwaltschaft. Der evangelische Publizist Robert Geisendörfer. Leben, Werk und Wirkungen*, Erlangen: Christliche-Publizistik-Verl.

Stapf, Ingrid (2006), *Medien-Selbstkontrolle: Ethik und Institutionalisierung*, Konstanz: UVK-Verl.-Ges.

Thomas, Günter (2004), Umkämpfte Aufmerksamkeit. Medienethische Erwägungen zu einer knappen kulturellen Ressource, in: *Zeitschrift für Evangelische Ethik* 47, pp. 89–104.

Türcke, Christoph (2009), *Philosophie des Traums*, München: Beck.

Utzschneider, Helmut (2007), *Gottes Vorstellung. Untersuchungen zur literarischen Ästhetik und ästhetischen Theologie des Alten Testaments*, Stuttgart: Kohlhammer.

Waldenfels, Bernhard (2005), *Phänomenologie der Aufmerksamkeit*, Frankfurt am Main: Suhrkamp.

Intercultural education and the media
– an educational perspective

Horst Niesyto

1. An approach to intercultural education

Since the late 1990s intercultural media education has become a focal point in media pedagogy. It is a response to the cultural pluralism of society, increased globalisation of media communication (especially through the internet), hopes raised for greater participation and exchange among individuals of different cultures, and issues of migration and social inequality. There has been a growing realisation that the cultural diversity of children and adolescents calls for a greater variety of educational opportunity. Intercultural education has developed a conceptual framework whose aim is sensitivity to difference both in respect of cultural diversity and of different age and social groups.

It is true that the concept of "education for diversity" (cf. e.g. Gogolin/Krüger-Potratz 2006) has become increasingly relevant to academic discourse in the past ten or twenty years but it is still quite far from being put into the everyday routine of education. Many teachers still have little knowledge of the lives and media worlds of children and adolescents from migration backgrounds. If, in addition, basic working conditions at schools involve large classes there is limited scope for responding to individual pupils or for introducing project-related activity. Intercultural education and intercultural learning call for practical experiences, the time to appreciate other people and things and to examine one's own patterns of interpretation and behaviour (Holzbrecher 2004). It is when children and young people are disadvantaged in their access to social, cultural and financial resources, that greater effort is required through education to give them experiences of self-worth and self-efficacy.

In considering the ideas behind intercultural education two approaches can be identified: the pedagogy of encounter and conflict-oriented intercultural education (cf. Nieke 2000, p. 36). *Pedagogy of encounter* aims to promote intercultural exchange between individuals and groups, especially members of cultural majority and minority groups, and envisages forms of intercultural communication across linguistic and national boundaries, e.g. in the context of seminars of encounter.

The primary aim of *conflict-oriented intercultural education* is to combat xenophobia, racism and ethnocentrism through a pedagogy committed to equality of opportunity for all members of society. Particular attention is paid to conflict and its associated viewpoints, judgements and stereotypes. Whichever approach is preferred, both concepts focus on the intercultural *processes of communication*. These processes of communication aim to develop a consciousness of cultural influence, to explore one's own experience of foreignness and to promote empathy, recognition and respect for other cultures. The opportunity to experience similarity does not mean ignoring or blurring difference. For Auernheimer (2003, p. 22) the predominant themes of intercultural education are: commitment to the equality of all, of whatever background; respectful attitude towards otherness; capacity for intercultural understanding; capacity for intercultural dialogue.

2. Media and migration – research findings

It is important when developing ideas of intercultural media education to consider evidence from research. Studies in recent years have concentrated on the area of the media and migration, and they reveal that a digital divide in the sense of a "parallel media society" between the native and immigrant populations does not exist (ARD/ZDF-Study *Migranten und Medien* 2007; cf. Simon 2007). Children and young people in a context of migration are no more a homogenous group than children and young people in general (Treibel et al. 2006). Different educational, social and cultural resources and priorities should be borne in mind when structuring intercultural media education activities.

Nevertheless, despite the diversity of issues and groups researched, certain similar *findings* emerged in different research projects (Hugger/ Hoffmann 2006; Moser et al. 2007; Niesyto/ Holzwarth/ Maurer 2007):

– Children and young people with a migrant background generally have a broader spectrum of response than non-migrants and draw on a variety of resources in their (receptive) media appropriation as well as in active media creation: media from their country of origin, global (usually English language) media services, as well as those in their country of immigration.
– Multiple media-cultural identity is expressed through both linguistic and non-linguistic means.
– Media services are essential to the process of developing a sense of orientation and identity, not in a rigid pattern, but stage-related and temporary; the

media do not cause identity diffusion – rather, they contribute productively to the managing of age-appropriate responsibilities.
- The internet is a communications forum used by many young people as a translocal medium of youth culture for self-discovery and engagement with others; comparable experiences of socialisation and socio-cultural affiliations lead to more intensive modes of internet communication, such as sharing experiences of diverse cultural identities.
- Non-linguistic forms of expression (the use of pictures, music) in projects for intercultural media communication and media production have enormous potential for new forms of transcultural communication.

The evidence suggests that intercultural media projects ought to take special note of presentative-symbolic forms of expression and communication. According to Langer (1987) presentative symbols such as gestures, music or images – in contrast to representative symbols – do not need any explanation or interpretation on a discursive level, but are directly understandable and effective. Presentative symbolism thus is capable of extending our conception of rationality as it conveys experience in a different way, based on holistic and at the same time symbolic processes. Langer's premise is that people convey their feelings and life experiences in symbolic form and not only through the vocabulary and syntax of *discursive* language. The significance of non-discursive sign systems (pictures, sounds, music, body language), she argues, is often undervalued.

Innovative forms of intercultural communication should start with the quality of visual and other presentational symbols in order to overcome the limitations of written and spoken forms. This is especially so where media-mediated interpretative paradigms increasingly influence our perception and experience of reality. It is not a case of setting visual language against the written and spoken word, but rather of *extending* the mode of intercultural communication, of examining and testing possibilities and limitations.

3. Aims of intercultural media education

Ours is a comprehensively mediatised society – not only for entertainment, information and communication, but also for education, learning, self-expression and life challenges. The main purpose of intercultural media education is to respond to experiences of foreignness, including experiences in media use: "on the one hand media are part of our everyday world, on the other media experience helps us to interpret the world" (Röll 2001, p. 81). The religious education academic Manfred L. Pirner expresses a similar view in his "Media Culture Approach to Religious Education" highlighting the close connection between media experience, real life and the world of Christian symbols (Pirner 2001; 2009). Intercultural literacy acknowledges the viewpoint of the subject and builds on existing knowledge, experiences and media competences, which are then a basis for further experiential and learning processes. As the aim is to critically examine common modes of thinking and open up new perspectives on the world, appropriate pedagogical (or media-educational) strategies are required.

General intentions and aims for a model of intercultural media education:

– create connections with daily life using media for processing experiences in different cultural and social contexts;
– creative symbol-based self-expression using visual and audio-visual media where the spoken and written word is inadequate;
– engage with what is foreign, new or unfamiliar in media self-productions;
– take part in public communication through completed media production presentations (local public venues, community broadcasts, internet)
– reinforce feelings of self-worth and self-efficacy;
– promote social learning;
– reflect on one's own patterns of cultural interpretation; including response to aesthetic experience;
– develop media-critical competence, e.g. in relation to the way media culture patterns tend to stereotype foreigners.

4. Activity types and examples of intercultural education

In media education practice a number of institutions have established priority areas of intercultural activity. The activities range from productive-receptive film education, active media work (especially in out-of-school settings), media teaching projects in schools (e.g. language learning) to intercultural support services and internet portals. *Active media work*, in particular, resulted in many projects and activities. The JFC Media Centre in Cologne undertook the task of creating a project network starting with the *Cross-Culture-Initiative* which was followed by further intercultural media projects by young people, such as hip hop workshops and many media, music and dance projects, all part of the international *ROOTS & ROUTES* network (cf. www.jfc.info and www.rootsnroutes. eu). Since then the theoretical underpinning and practical experiences of intercultural education have been set out in many brochures, books and also material available on the internet (e.g. Hugger/ Hoffmann 2006; Maurer 2004;

Ministerium für Frauen, Jugend, Familie und Gesundheit des Landes NRW 2000; Niesyto 2003; JFC Medienzentrum Köln 2002 and 2011).

4.1 Self-production through photos and video

Marrying *audio, visual and audio-visual* forms of expression and communication presents a special opportuity. Presentative-symbolic illustration through pictures and music is especially suitable for connecting with inner images, expressing feelings and helping to overcome language barriers. In the light of the global reach of media communication there is a wide array of symbolic meanings capable of being communicated across cultures, as well as culture-specific symbol systems (cf. the research project *VideoCulture*, Niesyto 2003; Niesyto/Buckingham/Fisherkeller 2003). Those responsible for intercultural education should exploit this potential even more.

– Photos and video enable people to see themselves and their world from outside, from another's perspective.
– Photos and video are low-threshold, fun and self-reflective simulations for exploring identity: How do I look in this pose? And in this outfit? Self-presentation, self-portrayal and self-discovery are important needs in adolescence.
– Pictures can easily be sent as e-mail attachments or via social media technologies. This is important in projects where young people communicate at a distance; for example, for virtual communication following a youth exchange.
– Where command of language is limited processes of reflection such as contemplation, narration, discussion and writing are more easily initiated through photos and video (cf. Tomforde / Holzwarth 2006).

Experience of media education shows that *active media work* is particularly helpful for thinking about and understanding the media. Digital technology has opened up new opportunities for production (more accurate and practical video editing), for distribution (photos and video on web-based platforms reach a wider public) and for reception and communication (interactive weblogs). By working with media young people engage in a learning process, achieve a product that can be shown, and experience the approval of others and a sense of self-efficacy. Approaches to *cultural* media education using a creative mix of media, music and physical expression have a proven track record in youth media work (e.g. hip hop and dance media projects).

The *working principles* which have proved most useful are:

– to focus on genres familiar to young people;
– to promote experimental fun forms of media production;
– to use practical material to support verbal *and* visual explanation of media presentation options;
– to create balance between structure defined (by teachers) and openness (young people organise themselves);
– to provide sufficient mentors for both group and individual counselling/support (cf. Maurer 2004, Niesyto 2005).

In self-productions young producers draw on their media culture preferences when directing their own intentions for self-expression. Many teachers have dismissed such "media citation" and imitative processes as merely the use of cliché, eliminating meaning (desymbolisation). However, this does not explain the processing of symbols as understood from the subject's viewpoint, caught in the interplay between (pre-formed) social symbolism in the media, subjective accomplishment and appropriation, and socio-cultural milieux. Processing the symbols of one's environment was always associated with acts of imitation. Far from being worthless, they may be understood as processes of symbol incorporation of varying intensity, creativity and reflexivity. Educationally, this means the appropriate conditions to enable symbol creation as well as the development of aesthetic understanding; it becomes a reflexive process when spaces are opened up for experiencing symbol difference, not merely successive aesthetic impressions and experiences. Symbol creation becomes experience creation when perception of difference is acknowledged, when distance between the self and the environment is recognised and can be symbolically processed.

4.2 Active-receptive film education

Besides creating their own media productions, there are the well-tried traditions in educational programmes of *active-receptive film education* using popular feature films, television series and video productions. Media productions present images of otherness in concentrated form; film analysis makes it possible to reflect critically on media discourse about migration (positive and negative images and clichés about others). Examples of sources suitable for intercultural media education programmes are: *Youth4Media – European network association* (http://www.youth4media.eu/), *Cine-minis: Short French Films for Language Learning and Literacy* (http://filmstore.bfi.org.uk/acatalog/info_17774.html), *Festival of Animated Film* in Stuttgart (http://www.itfs.de/en/home/competitions/), CHICAM – Children in Communication about Migration (http://www.chicam.org/).

Watching and engaging with short films and feature films is a valuable approach to intercultural film education. Films with appeal and a closeness to real life such as *Kick it like Beckham* make the topic of migration and intercultural communication more accessible. Tasks requiring observation of content and filmic conventions produce interpretations which can be compared: for example, how are people with a background of migration portrayed? and those without a background of migration? How is the country of origin shown? and the country of immigration? How are women and men portrayed? What prejudices can be identified?

There is a variety of methodological approaches to film education where verbal communication is required:

– open or structured discussion;
– before the film allocate observation tasks and/or form "expert groups";
– "flash light": brief reactions from everyone;
– talk about favourite scenes;
– stop the film and elicit suggestions for what might come next;
– compare films from two different countries with migration theme and identify similarities and differences;
– discuss what can be inferred from the cover images.

In addition to different types of discussion, introducing alternative pedagogical methods as follow-up activities is strongly recommended. Some of these might be: artwork depicting key scenes; reconstruct a storyboard with individual images; create stills and use body language and mime to play scenes from the film; write pen portraits of the main characters; create a film poster or flyer from stills; put together a trailer from individual sequences; reaction to the film as starting point for own film production. Processes such as these can be linked to activities of selecting, comparing and planning to stimulate emotional distance and critical ability.

5. Perspectives of intercultural media education

There is still a *huge gap* between, on the one hand, general declarations of educational policy for the promotion of media competence and media literacy and, on the other, broad-based sustainable measures to enhance media-related education. Current debates on immigration and social inequality show that concentrating on systematic language acquisition does not go far enough to increase children and young people's opportunities for social participation. The *interaction* of various modes of self-expression, communication and adaptation to the world can help children and adolescents – especially those from disadvantaged backgrounds – to reinforce their existing strengths and potential, as empirical experience and many case studies have shown. This is an important task for schools and other centres of learning (see Holzwarth / Maurer / Niesyto 2006).

In this context the *Manifesto on Media Education* (http://www.keine-bildung-ohne-medien.de/manifesto-on-media-education/), which has already attracted over 1,300 signatures from individuals and organisations, calls for increased public funding to make a significant improvement in infrastructure and staffing levels.[1] The *basics* of media education ought to be a *compulsory* component in the professional training of pre-school teachers, teachers and those working in adult education and social work. The objectives of intercultural and media education cannot succeed in practice if teachers are not familiar with the real and media worlds of children and adolescents from diverse cultural and social backgrounds, and if they are not able or willing to develop ideas and activities appropriate to their teaching groups. Unfortunately many teachers, influenced by middle class media socialisation, continue to denigrate the popular culture media experiences of children and adolescents to the detriment of their educational development.

Given the ambivalent processes of media globalisation, an effective intercultural media science would not restrict itself to the topic of migration. In essence, the historic development of *region-specific* media cultures should not be overlooked; on the contrary, the way they contrast with, and interact with, global media formats can be analysed. An example would be the interaction of different global and local media within diverse culture groups. It is important that an understanding of *cultural difference* in media development should be acquired, especially through comparative analysis of orality, literacy and imagery, if projects on intercultural media education are to be developed and implemented with cultural sensitivity.

Finally: at a time when culture and media policy is framed increasingly from an economic perspective (economisation), the value of a media programmes and services cannot be measured solely by their popular success, user figures and sales. Media education must be supported by media policy and guarantee scope for a *wide range* of opportunities. It is not a matter of the state regulating the media; instead there should be greater public debate among people concerned

---

1   On European level similar initiatives are: http://www.declarationdebruxelles.be/, http://www. euromedialiteracy.eu/charter.php, and a collection of statements can be found at: http://www. manifestoformediaeducation.co.uk/

with the media: politicians, producers, journalists and teachers, for the purpose of greater diversity and programme quality. Central to this aim is an engagement with issues of media ethics for a stronger consciousness of human dignity, truthfulness and credibility.

References

Auernheimer, Georg (2003), *Einführung in die Interkulturelle Pädagogik*, Darmstadt: WBG.

Bonfadelli, Heinz / Moser, Heinz (ed.) (2007), *Medien und Migration. Europa als multikultureller Raum?* Wiesbaden: VS Verlag für Sozialwissenschaften.

Gogolin, Ingrid / Krüger-Potratz, Marianne (ed.) (2006), *Einführung in die Interkulturelle Pädagogik*, Opladen & Farmington Hills: UTB.

Holzbrecher, Alfred (2004), *Interkulturelle Pädagogik*, Berlin: Cornelsen Verlag Scriptor.

Holzwarth, Peter (2007), Rezeptive und produktive Formen interkultureller Medienpädagogik, in: Niesyto, Horst / Holzwarth, Peter / Maurer, Björn (eds.), *Interkulturelle Kommunikation mit Foto und Video. Ergebnisse des EU-Projekts "Children in Communication about Migration" (CHICAM)*, München: Kopäd.

Holzwarth, Peter / Maurer, Björn / Niesyto, Horst (2006), Media, migration and school. Visions for media education in intercultural settings, in: Baraldi, Claudio (Ed.): *Education and intercultural narratives in multicultural classrooms*, Rom: Officina, pp. 165–185.

Hugger, Kai-Uwe / Hoffmann, Dagmar (eds.) (2006), *Medienbildung in der Migrationsgesellschaft. GMK-Schriften zur Medienpädagogik 39*, Bielefeld: Gesellschaft für Medienpädagogik und Kommunikationskultur in der Bundesrepublik.

JFC Medienzentrum Köln (ed.) (2011), *Jugendmedienarbeit für kulturelle Vielfalt mit Video und Web 2.0*, Köln.

JFC Medienzentrum Köln (ed.) (2002), *Media Mix Mondial – Ideen für die interkulturelle Medienarbeit*, Zeitschrift MedienConcret, Themenheft 2002.

Langer, Susanne (1987, orig. 1942), *Philosophie auf neuem Wege*, Frankfurt/Main: Fischer-Taschenbuch-Verlag.

Maurer, Björn (2004), *Medienarbeit mit Kindern aus Migrationskontexten. Grundlagen und Praxisbausteine*, München: Kopäd.

Ministerium für Frauen, Jugend, Familie und Gesundheit des Landes Nordrhein-Westfalen (ed.) (2000), *Expertise "Interkulturelle Jugendmedienarbeit in NRW"*, Düsseldorf, Remscheid.

Nieke, Wolfgang (2000), *Interkulturelle Erziehung und Bildung. Wertorientierungen im Alltag*, Opladen: VS Verlag für Sozialwissenschaften.

Niesyto, Horst (ed.) (2003), *VideoCulture – Video und interkulturelle Kommunikation. Grundlagen, Methoden und Ergebnisse eines internationalen Forschungsprojekts*, München: Kopäd.

Niesyto, Horst (2005), *Chancen und Perspektiven interkultureller Medienpädagogik. Plenumsvortrag auf dem 22. GMK-Forum in Bielefeld*, online: http://www.ph-ludwigsburg.de/fileadmin/subsites/1b-mpxx-t-01/user_files/Niesyto_Interkulturelle-Medienpdagogik.pdf [27.06.2012]

Niesyto, Horst / Buckingham, David / Fisherkeller, Ellen (2003), VideoCulture: Crossing Borders with Young People's Video Productions, in: *Television & New Media* 4, No. 4, pp. 461–482.

Niesyto, Horst / Holzwarth, Peter / Maurer, Björn (2007), *Interkulturelle Kommunikation mit Foto und Video. Ergebnisse des EU-Projekts "Children in Communication about Migration" (CHICAM)*, München: Kopäd.

Pirner, Manfred L. (2001), *Fernsehmythen und religiöse Bildung. Grundlegung einer medienerfahrungsorientierten Religionspädagogik am Beispiel fiktionaler Fernsehunterhaltung*, Frankfurt/Main: Gemeinschaftswerk Ev. Publizistik.

Pirner, Manfred L. (2009), The Media Culture Approach to Religious Education. An Outline with a Focus on Interreligious Learning, in: Miedema, S. / Meijer, W. / Lanser-van der Velde, A. (eds.), *Religious Education in a World of Religious Diversity*, Münster/Berlin/New York/Munich: Waxmann, pp. 149–164.

Röll, Franz Josef (2001), Imagination und symbolorientierte Medienpädagogik, in: Belgrad, Jürgen / Niesyto, Horst (Ed.), *Symbol. Verstehen und Produktion in pädagogischen Kontexten*, Hohengehren: Schneider-Verl. Hohengehren, pp. 74–85.

Simon, Erik (2007), Migranten und Medien 2007, in: *Media Perspektiven* 11, No. 9, pp. 426–435.

Theunert, Helga (ed.) (2008), *Interkulturell mit Medien*, München: Kopäd.

Tomforde, Barbara / Holzwarth, Peter (2006), Das Wesentliche ist für die Augen unsichtbar...? Fotografie im interkulturellen Jugendaustausch, in: Holzbrecher, Alfred / Oomen-Welke, Ingelore / Schmolling, Jan (eds.), *Photographs + Text. Handbuch für die Bildungsarbeit*, Wiesbaden: VS Verlag für Sozialwissenschaften, pp. 369–373.

Treibel, Annette / Maier, Maja .S. / Kommer, Sven / Welzel, Manuela (eds.) (2006), *Gender medienkompetent. Medienbildung in einer heterogenen Gesellschaft*, Wiesbaden: VS Verlag für Sozialwissenschaften.

Media culture and interreligious learning
– a religious education perspective

Manfred L. Pirner

In the teaching about world religions and interreligious learning the media have received little attention up till now, and then mainly in the form of practical advice on teaching with multimedia. This can be exemplified by the comprehensive "International Handbook of Inter-religious Education" (Engebretson et al. 2010). It contains one contribution on "Promoting Interfaith Education through ICT" (Gross 2010) that deals with the instrumental use of electronic media for teaching, but the eminent role of media culture in shaping and influencing the image of religion and religions in Western societies does not come into the focus of the handbook.

This is a somewhat surprising finding given that much of the international research contained in this volume shows clearly that today's media culture is of great significance for religions and for interreligious understanding. I am concerned here with the public, mainly electronic media, and if I use the shorthand of "media culture" I am referring primarily to the electronic mass media and their content.

Before examining how they affect religious education and interreligious learning, I would like to clarify how interreligious learning can be conceptualised in the context of the philosophy of education.

1. What is interreligious learning? Reflections from educational theory

To my mind, one of the most convincing modern views of religious education in the context of the philosophy of education is given by Bernhard Dressler. Bernhard Dressler's central idea is that religious education depends on being able to alternate between an internal religious perspective and an external perspective; the change of perspective being between "speaking religiously" and "speaking about religion" (Dressler 2006, p. 94; cf. also Dressler 2012), between taking part in cultural and communicative practice (participation) and observing, considering, evaluating this practice (reflection). Children and young people have to learn both: they should at least have an idea of what a lived religion is; they should be enabled to take part in it, if that is what they want, and they should be able to think and evaluate critically the role of religion in their lives, in other people's lives and in our society.

Dressler places this view of religious education within the general pedagogical concept of different ways of accessing the world, or what Jürgen Baumert (2002) calls "modes of encountering the world". In this context encountering the world through religion is (together with philosophy, which also addresses "problems of constitutive rationality") different from, and not to be equated with, other modes such as the natural sciences or art and aesthetics. For Dressler each mode of accessing the world involves the dialectics of participation and reflection or, to use Niklas Luhmann's expression, of first-order and second-order observation. For example, physics takes a characteristic scientific view of the world (the world is observed from the viewpoint of physics); at the same time physics education includes the knowledge that this perspective is one among others. The characteristic second-order observation is how physics apprehends the world and makes a model or construct of it. Dressler considers it important for education generally, and for religious education in particular, that students should learn to distinguish between the different ways of accessing the world, but also to alternate between, and form connections among, them.

In this context it is important to note that religion, in itself, educates. In other words, accessing the world through religion has a strong correlation with education because religious spirituality helps one to see oneself, and the world, from an external perspective. Asking about God and about the whole purpose and meaning of my life helps to distance me from my immediate situation, allowing me to take a bird's eye view – or God's eye view – of myself and my life. This distancing from the self, or from the world, literally opens up new perspectives of perception and judgement. From a Christian theological point of view Henning Luther sums up religion as "distance from the world" (Luther 1992, p. 25); Dietrich Korsch describes religious competence as a "competence for difference" in one's life, "the ability to interpret oneself, that is, a distancing from the self which enables a return to the self" (Korsch 2004, p. 17).

I shall now expand a little beyond Dressler and show how the interreligious dimension of religious education fits into this concept. Following his basic approach we find that at the heart of meaningful learning about so-called "foreign" religions is this alternation of internal and external perspective. Dressler himself shows that today for many students in Christian RE Christianity is a foreign religion, and that it must be assumed that many of them are neither religious nor believers. Yet, these non-believer students should also be encouraged to explore a Christian faith perspective and, in so doing, try out an internal perspective of religion. The same goes for learning about other religions in Christian RE and for students who confess to be believers and to belong to a particular religion.

I well remember 10th grade high-school students coming to me at the end of an RE lesson on Buddhism saying, "Herr Pirner, are you actually trying to convert us to Buddhism?" I took the question as a compliment, because my lesson had obviously succeeded in giving a comprehensible and attractive picture of Buddhism from an internal perspective, which had really confused my Christian students in their Protestant RE class. At least it had given them an inkling of what Buddhism is all about. An internal perspective is indispensable for religious education and best delivered, of course, by a representative of the particular religion. However, it is part of the professionalism of religious education teachers – including denominational RE classes – to put themselves in the position of other religions with empathy and understanding and convey the internal perspective as comprehensibly as possible.

At the same time, the context of religious pluralism generates the awareness that a specific religious perspective is one among others. It is by encountering other religions or world views that an external perspective on one's own religion or world view can develop. A Christian encountering Islam, for example, realises that his Christian perspective is not the only possible or meaningful interpretation of life, the world and reality. And it is also true that, through encounter with religion(s), those with non-religious or atheist leanings can realise that their "god-less" view of the world is not the only possible one. Experiences like these urge and promote reflection: How do Islamic and Christian perspectives relate to each other? How do religious and atheist perspectives relate to one another? In a case of conflict, how can one judge which perspective is the more appropriate, the more true? Consequently, in an educational theory perspective encounter with other religions and world views is to be encouraged precisely because it stimulates, supports and promotes reflective education.

This, however, also requires intensive study of one's own internal religious or world-view perspective, because it is primarily from this internal perspective that I view and evaluate the perception that my religion or world view is not the only one. This evaluation implies two aspects: The first is that the other religion is *de facto* in competition to my own in the field of general interpretative frameworks searching for the truth of life and reality. The second is that, unlike other modes of encountering the world my religion and other religions reveal 'family resemblances' (Wittgenstein). It is therefore possible that people with a strong faith or world view will have a better understanding and appreciation of a different religion or world view from their own than people unconcerned with either. As a result, different religions may find themselves allies in defending the right to access the world through religion against those challenging that basic assumption.

But when the emphasis is on competition alone, and the internal perspective rejects the idea of religious pluralism, then this raises fundamental barriers and is an obstacle to education. Karl Ernst Nipkow was right to emphasise so strongly that, if interreligious understanding and interreligious learning are to stand a chance, religious persons must be able to value and appreciate religious pluralism from their own internal religious perspective (cf. Nipkow 1998).

I would like to follow another train of thought here. In the context of social and religious pluralism, the external perspective is not just an abstraction which lets me perceive my own religion or world view as one among others. Rather, the external perspective is a multiple one; that is, it sheds the light of a number of external perspectives on my own religion. It lets me see, for example, how psychology or sociology views religion generally, and my religion in particular. And I learn how a different religion views my religion; how, for example, Christianity is viewed from the perspective of Judaism, Islam or the Bahá'í faith. This engages further reflective, educational processes which require me to renew my understanding of my own religion by exploring the external perspectives I encounter. A religion that willingly and competently faces this challenge to take into account perspectives from other religions and world views can be enriched and gain a deeper self-understanding. Such a religion could be called a reflective or educated religion.

As a conclusion we can say that frequent change between internal and external perspective(s) is a vital component of religious and interreligious education. The ability to accomplish such change of perspective is the essence of religious and interreligious competence. And: an 'educated religion' denotes one that is ready and able to relate external perspectives critically and constructively to its internal perspectives, possibly to the point of integration.

In this context of religious education, how is the role of electronic media to be understood?

2. Media and interreligious learning from the perspective of educational theory

2.1. Media and education

First of all, accessing the world through media has, as we have noted in the case of religion, a strong correlation with education, because a vital component of media reality is the dialectic between internal and external perspectives, between representation and distance, between participation and reflection. Media bring what is far away or unfamiliar close to us, enabling participation and empathy, and put what is familiar and near at an unfamiliar distance so that we see it "with different eyes". Media reception research examines the alternation between media and non-media reality which is a characteristic of the way audiences interact with media realities (cf., for example, Mikos 1994, p. 81). When I watch a film I can enter its internal perspective and "be there", but I can also exit at will and think my own thoughts about the presentation of the theme, the performance of the actors or the camera work.

In particular, public media reinforce external perspectives of religion and religions by promoting pluralisation and globalisation and thus broadening our horizon. By introducing varied, strange, unfamiliar ways of life from far-off countries they contribute significantly to multicultural and multi-religious experience. Even if someone in Europe has never actually met a Jewish person, they will have seen pictures on television of "Jewish settlers in the West Bank", or of ultra-orthodox Jews at the Wailing Wall in Jerusalem. The world-wide reaction to the Danish Muhammad cartoons would have scarcely been conceivable without television or the internet, nor the controversy caused by German Chancellor Merkel at the ceremony honouring the Danish cartoonist. These instances show the media pressing for interreligious issues and promoting interreligious discourse. The media demand and promote education – in particular religious education and a critical media education that addresses questions about the truth and reality of media images.

2.2 Media and religion I: why media culture resembles religion

Not only has media culture a strong correlation with education, it has also a strong correlation with religion. Public media, like religion, are observers of virtually the whole world and the whole of our lives. The big questions about our lives – where we have come from, where we are going, about destiny, love and death – are the major stuff of media narratives and, at the same time, the central questions of religion. To this extent for many people in the West the media are a kind of religion or religion substitute. Many young people looking for meaning and direction in their lives find them, not in traditional religions, but in the media – a development established in a number of empirical studies (cf. Pirner 2009a; 2009b; 2011b).

In this respect media culture is competing with religions in endeavouring to explain the realities of life and the world; it has, on the one hand, become something of an ersatz religion and is certainly partly responsible for the loss of status among the traditional, institutional religions. On the other hand, the religion-like

131

status of the media is also capable of acting as a bridge to religion: by sensitising people to existential, ethical and religious questions and dimensions of life and thereby making them receptive to religious interpretation and practice. Media reality can convey the sense that there is something "over and above" our everyday reality; it can act as a common reference point or language, a "lingua franca", across the divide of religion or culture. For example, empirical evidence suggests that young Muslims in Germany find hip hop helps integration (cf. Lübcke 2007; for more details on the lingua-franca function of the media see Pirner 2009c).

2.3 Media and religion II: religion as content of the media culture

Media culture offers chances for the religions to portray themselves and their internal perspective; above all, though, they see themselves portrayed from many other external perspectives. News reports, commentaries and internet pages spotlight religions and world views from all possible angles and aspects. Popular fictional stories and advertising messages frequently use, and often transform, elements, symbols and narratives from religious tradition (cf. Pirner 2001; Buschmann/Pirner 2003). The same happens with the relationship of religions to each other or their dealings with one another. For religious education this presents opportunities as well as challenges. Religious education can start with the presence of religion in media culture and from there disclose the backgrounds, origins and roots of religious traditions and perspectives. When religion is transformed or distorted in the media this can and should be subjected to critical analysis – an analysis that should extend to the functions and mechanisms of the media, as well as the commercial and power interests in the background. Religious education and media education thus can and should go hand in hand.

To sum up, this viewpoint from educational theory sees a major task in the field of media and religion to help children and young people to distinguish between different realities or modes of accessing the world – those of the media and religion –, to discover or create multiple connections between them and develop the ability to assess these connections critically.

3. Media and interreligious learning – a perspective from socialisation theory

For all that I have certainly gained from Bernhard Dressler's approach to educational theory, I have to question some of his premises from socialisation theory and what they reveal about his concept of religion. With regard to religion and religious socialisation, Dressler tends to the view that children and young people are "tabulae rasae", blank slates, with little idea of religion, the principal task for teachers of religion being to act as tourist guide introducing them to a foreign country (cf. Dressler 2009, p. 124).[1] Similar views about the socialisation of to-day's younger generation can be found in numerous religious education pro-grammes and publications. I would not deny that young people are less familiar than ever with biblical and Christian traditions, and that the very unfamiliarity of Christianity can present school students with a fresh stimulus and challenge to find out about the unknown. But if this view becomes over-dominant there is a risk that too narrow an understanding of religion will lead to an educational defi-cit model that views children and young people only or primarily as exhibiting a deficiency which must be remediated by the religious education teacher. By contrast, if we employ a wider concept of religion, we may discover that many young people, although not familiar with biblical or Christian traditions, have their own ways and languages to reflect on and communicate about God, faith and the existential questions of life. And even if they are without contact to a re-ligious community they may have encountered many cultural elements of relig-ion in popular media culture and use the language codes and symbols of pop mu-sic or of fantasy and science fiction films to exchange ideas on existential, ethical and religious themes. This is exactly what recent empirical studies on youth cul-tures and on the language young people use reveal, as will be demonstrated be-low. For educational as well as theological reasons pedagogical approaches that appreciate and value young people's own resources and skills should be pre-ferred to a deficit pedagogy or model. It seems important to apply the principle "There is no child who cannot do anything, who has nothing useful or interesting to tell [...]" (Lähnemann 2005, p. 413) also to the field or religious education – and to media education as well. As many teachers know from experience, chil-dren and young people often display skills in the field of electronic and digital media which surpass the skills of their teachers.

The idea of the pupils as "tabulae rasae" presents a problem, above all be-cause it disregards forms of informal learning from contexts other than family and community. For the particular area of interreligious learning, Karl Ernst Nipkow has rightly emphasised the importance of informal learning and in this context has also referred to forms of youth culture and media (Nipkow 2005, pp. 367ff.).

---

1   It is not the place here to analyse Dressler's concept of religion in detail. Nevertheless, there seems to me to be a certain tension between a narrow, phenomenological, more substantive un-derstanding of religion, where he is concerned didactically with "showing" religion, and a broader, more functional understanding of religion in the context of educational theory.

To sum up: children and young people live their lives today, to a substantial degree, in the world of media. Their socialisation is largely a media socialisation. This, and the way the media are used in young people's peer groups and in youth cultures without the involvement of educational institutions, and mostly without adult educational accompaniment, is often termed in the sociology of childhood and youth the "self-socialisation" of adolescents by and with media (cf. Abels/König 2010, pp. 229ff.; Rhein/Müller 2006; Pirner 2004; Zinnecker 2000). Religious and interreligious learning are part of this self-socialisation and therefore to be given consideration in the processes of intentional teaching and learning. Two empirically documented examples will demonstrate this religious self-socialisation.

The first example is from the popular television science fiction series "Star Trek". It shows a world in the distant future in which intelligent life in human-like form has already been discovered on many other planets. The peoples of these planets have learned by and large to get along peacefully with one another and to respect their differences. An important role is played by varied forms of religion and spirituality, and a recurring principle of the plot is respect for the other religion and a willingness to take from it something that may inform one's own religious or non-religious world view (cf. Hellmann/Klein 1997; Buchholz 1998). An empirical study of Star Trek fans conducted at the University of Bonn found that many of them, too, placed a high value on tolerance for other, unfamiliar ways of life and faith (Volkskundliches Seminar 2006).

The second example is of the goths, members of a subculture sometimes also referred to as the black scene, who stand out because of their preference for wearing black and for their emphasis on death and transience. In this youth culture, media, especially certain forms of pop and rock music, play an important role. In an empirical study we interviewed young adults on this scene (Sprio 2008; Pirner 2011a), and were able to confirm the result of an existing study (Schmidt/Neumann-Braun 2008) that a major characteristic of the scene is thinking deeply about things. Those involved reject a shallow culture of having fun, playing hard and looking beautiful. The conventional taboos in society, talking about death, transience and religion, are no taboos in the gothic youth culture; goths think deeply about religious matters, including showing tolerance towards those with different religious or non-religious leanings. Below are two examples from the interviews:

"Sure, there are Christians here too, and there aren't many who believe in nothing at all. O.k., not necessarily in God, but in ghosts or something. [...]" (Sprio 2008, p. 38; Sina, 20J.)

"What is also a general characteristic [of gothic culture] is that people are looking for something that's not just up there or down here, something you can't touch or see, something science can't prove. Everybody's looking for something different. [...] It doesn't have to be Jesus Christ, but it could be, and there are people who say, that it is for me, but I'm still a goth [...]" (Schmidt/Neumann-Braun 2008, p. 245; Manfred, Passage 27).

I don't deny that these statements show signs of a syncretism that may be regarded as being problematic. But at least one can welcome, pedagogically and theologically, the underlying trend of thoughtful tolerance, or tolerant thoughtfulness which goes against superficiality and dismissing religion outright. It is striking how the goth scene has developed its own symbolic language allowing communication on existential and religious matters. This language certainly draws on tradition, including religious tradition, but it also has something self-contained about it. In a recent empirical study on young people's language use Stefan Altmeyer has shown that, even for youngsters not affiliated to a religious community, religion is not a "foreign language" and it is therefore wrong to describe them as "religiously speechless" (Altmeyer 2011).

I am convinced that religious education, especially when the aim is interreligious learning, should take seriously the experience and skills young people already possess, often acquired through informal processes of self-socialisation, and use them as a pedagogical starting point. In this view, a key task for religious education is to accompany eductionally the religious (self-)socialisation of children and young people. School education is, above all, effective, if it impacts on the students' self-socialisation and enhances their non-formal learning experience in their everyday life world. If students have studied in religious education classes the way religions are portrayed by the media, and take this on board in their everyday media experience with a different, more discriminating, more critical eye, then this would be a positive impact. Such an approach to religious education will most probably succeed if elements of media education are built in to religious education syllabuses.

In conclusion I would like to express these ideas in terms of five guidelines for religious education practice, with reference to associated and desirable competences.

4. Media and interreligious learning – five guidelines for educational practice

1. Do not think of children and young people as "blank slates" with little idea of religion and, at best, able to ask questions or seek answers (deficit model). Think of them rather as "experts" of their daily (media) lives, who have already reflected by themselves on existential, religious and interreligious questions and

who have already found some answers (resources model). Help them to develop their personal resources constructively and self-critically (in the sense of accompanying their self-socialisation educationally) and in so doing to discover the life-enriching potential of religion(s) as part of, or apart from, the media culture – but also to become aware of the life-endangering risks of religion(s) (perceptual competence) .

2. Do not think of children and young people as religiously "speechless". Anticipate, rather, that even secular adolescents may make use of elements of a (symbolic) language from media culture with which to reflect on and discuss issues of existential, ethical and religious scope. Incorporate media elements in religious education classes to improve communication with students – especially those with less language skills. With the help of religious traditions, support them in acquiring more thoughtful, discriminating, reflective competences of religious expression, communication and thinking.

3. Do not think of children and young people as just passive consumers of media culture, helplessly exposed to its manipulative influences, but rather as active, constructive, if often vulnerable, media users. Think of religious education classes as an opportunity to reveal the distortions and bias in the way religions are portrayed by the media, and to foster a culture of media use in which media and content are perceived in a more nuanced, critical way, and used more creatively and autonomously (perceptual, interpretative and creative competences).

4. Do not construct a contradiction between the primary experiences of direct social encounter and the seemingly secondary experiences of the world of media. Show young people valuable alternatives to media consumption as well as valuable alternatives to the general superficiality of media. Support them in finding orientation in Christianity or other religions so as to engage critically and constructively with the media and to develop their skills of judgement about the media and non-media world (evaluative competence).

5. Do not refer to media culture in a generalised, disparaging way; remember that, in order to "function", neither religions nor democratic societies (nor religious and interreligious dialogue in them) can dispense with the media. Grasp the opportunity of the contribution media cultures make to intercultural and interreligious understanding; help young people to media and religious competence and to take part in religious, interreligious and social communication (participatory and creative competences).

References

Abels, Heinz / König, Alexandra (2010), *Sozialisation*, Wiesbaden: VS-Verlag.

Altmeyer, Stefan (2011), *Fremdsprache Religion? Sprachempirische Studien im Kontext religiöser Bildung*, Stuttgart: Kohlhammer.

Baumert, Jürgen (2002), Deutschland im internationalen Bildungsvergleich, in: N. Killius / J. Kluge / L. Reisch (eds*), Die Zukunft der Bildung*, Frankfurt am Main: Suhrkamp, pp. 100–150.

Buchholz, Martin (1998), *Dokumentar-Film: Messias im Raumschiff. Der Science-fiction-Kult.*

Buschmann, Gerd / Pirner, Manfred L. (2003), *Werbung – Religion – Bildung*, Frankfurt am Main: GEP.

Dressler, Bernhard (2006), *Unterscheidungen. Religion und Bildung*, Leipzig: Evang. Verlags-Anstalt.

Dressler, Bernhard (2009), Was soll eine gute Religionslehrerin, ein guter Religionslehrer können?, in: *Theo-Web. Zeitschrift für Religionspädagogik* 8, H. 2, pp. 115–127 (www.theo-web.de).

Dressler, Bernhard (2012), "Religiös reden" und "über Religion reden" lernen – Religionsdidaktik als Didaktik des Perspektivenwechsels, in: Grümme/Lenhard/Pirner, pp. 68–78.

Engebretson, Kath / de Souza, Marian / Durka, Gloria / Gearon, Liam (eds.) (2010), *International Handbook of Inter-religious Education*, 2 vol., Dordrecht/Heidelberg/London/New York: Springer.

Gross, Zehavit (2010), Promoting Interfaith Education through ICT – A Case Study, in: Engebretson et al., pp. 377–388.

Grümme, Bernhard / Lenhard, Hartmut / Pirner, Manfred L. (eds.) (2012), *Religionsunterricht neu denken. Innovative Ansätze und Perspektiven der Religionsdidaktik. Ein Arbeitsbuch für Studierende und Lehrer/innen*, Stuttgart: Kohlhammer.

Hellmann, Kai-Uwe / Klein, Arne (eds.) (1997), *"Unendliche Weiten [...]" – Star Trek zwischen Unterhaltung und Utopie*, Frankfurt a.M.: Fischer Taschenbuchverlag.

Korsch, Dietrich (2004), Wie bildet sich Religion? Über "Lehre" und "Verkündigung" bei ReligionslehrerInnen, in: Dressler, B. / Feige, A. / Schöll, A. (eds.), *Religion – Leben, Lernen, Lehren. Ansichten zur "Religion" bei ReligionslehrerInnen (Grundlegungen 9)*, Münster: LIT, pp. 17–28.

Lähnemann, Johannes (2005), Lernergebnisse: Kompetenzen und Standards interreligiösen Lernens, in: Schreiner, P. / Sieg, U. / Elsenbast, V. (eds.), *Handbuch Interreligiöses Lernen*, Gütersloh: Gütersloher Verlaghaus, pp. 409–421.

Lübcke, Claudia (2007), Jugendkulturen junger Muslime in Deutschland, in: Wensierski, Hans-Jürgen von / Lübcke, Claudia (eds.), *Junge Muslime in Deutschland*, Opladen: Budrich, pp. 285–318.

Luther, Henning (1992), *Religion und Alltag. Bausteine zu einer praktischen Theologie des Subjekts*, Stuttgart: Radius-Verlag.

Mikos, Lothar (1994), *Fernsehen im Erleben der Zuschauer*, Berlin: Quintessenz.

Nipkow, Karl Ernst (1998), *Bildung in einer pluralen Welt, vol. 2. Religionspädagogik im Pluralismus*, Gütersloh: Gütersloher Verlagshaus.

Nipkow, Karl Ernst (2005), Ziele interreligiösen Lernens als mehrdimensionales Problem, in: Schreiner, P. / Sieg, U. / Elsenbast, V. (eds), *Handbuch Interreligiöses Lernen*, Gütersloh: Gütersloher Verlagshaus, pp. 362–380.

Pirner, Manfred L. (2001), *Fernsehmythen und religiöse Bildung*, Frankfurt a.M.: GEP.

Pirner, Manfred L. (2004), Selbstsozialisation – Zur pädagogischen Tragfähigkeit eines soziologischen Konzepts, in: *Online-Magazin "Ludwigsburger Beiträge zur Medienpädagogik"* 5, pp. 13–16.

Pirner, Manfred L. (2009a), Religious Socialization by the Media? An Empirical Study and Conclusions for Practical Theology, in: *International Journal of Practical Theology* 13, No. 2, pp. 275–292.

Pirner, Manfred L. (2009b), Religion, in: Vollbrecht, Ralf / Wegener, Claudia (eds.), *Handbuch Mediensozialisation*, Wiesbaden: VS-Verlag für Sozialwissenschaft, pp. 294–301.

Pirner, Manfred L. (2009c), The Media Culture Approach to Religious Education. An Outline with a Focus on Interreligious Learning, in: Miedema, S. / Meijer, W. / Lanser-van der Velde, A. (eds.), *Religious Education in a World of Religious Diversity*, Münster/Berlin/New York/Munich: Waxmann, pp. 149–164.

Pirner, Manfred L. (2011a), Religiöse und politische Selbstsozialisation. Wahrnehmungen und Herausforderungen am Beispiel der Gothic-Jugendszene, in: Benedict, H.-J. / Engelschalk, A. / Pirner, M. L. (eds.), "Hey, Mr. President [...]". *Politik und populäre Kultur. Sozialwissenschaftliche und theologische Perspektiven*, Jena: IKS Garamond, pp. 123–145.

Pirner, Manfred L. (2011b), Peer Group and Media Influence on Young People in their (Non-)Religious Development. A Christian Perspective, in: El Bouayadi-van de Wetering, Stella / Miedema, Siebren (eds.), *Reaching for the Sky. Religious Education from Christian and Islamic Perspectives*, Amsterdam / New York: Rodopi, pp. 205–222.

Rhein, Stefanie / Müller, Renate (2006), Musikalische Selbstsozialisation Jugendlicher: Theoretische Perspektiven und Forschungsergebnisse, in: *Diskurs Kindheits- und Jugendforschung* 4/2006, pp. 551–568.

Schmidt, Axel / Neumann-Braun, Klaus (2008), *Die Welt der Gothics. Spielräume düster konnotierter Tranzendenz*, 2nd ed., Wiesbaden: VS-Verlag.

Sprio, David (2008). *Religiöse Aspekte in der Jugendkultur des Goth. Pädagogische Herausforderungen für den Religionsunterricht in Realschulen.* Wissenschaftliche Hausarbeit zur Ersten Staatsprüfung für das Lehramt an Realschulen an der PH Ludwigsburg.

Tworuschka, Udo (2006), Forschungsstelle religionsvermittelnde Medien, in: P. Schreiner / U. Sieg / V. Elsenbast (eds), *Handbuch Interreligiöses Lernen*, Gütersloh: Gütersloher Verlagshaus, pp. 682–684.

Volkskundliches Seminar der Universität Bonn (2005). Bericht über eine empirische Studie unter Star Trek Fans unter: www.uni-bonn.de/Aktuelles/Presseinformationen/2005/417.html (download: 24.10.2006).

Zinnecker, Jürgen (2000), Selbstsozialisation – Essay über ein aktuelles Konzept, in: *Zeitschrift für Soziologie der Erziehung und Sozialisation* 20, H. 3, pp. 272–290.

Religion in journalism.
A proposal of ethical standards

Daniel Meier / Peter Philipp

Introduction

In recent years the reporting of "religion" has become increasingly controversial. Journalists are caught, especially in respect of Islam, between conflicting issues which are passionately debated in the media, not primarily because of religion itself but because of the abuse of religion by politicians, ideologues and violent extremists for political and ideological ends. For this reason such reporting is covered primarily by specialists in foreign and security affairs and regional affairs (Middle East, Arab world) rather than by specialists in religion. Domestically, Islam is a topic usually handled by experts in migration, immigration and integration who by and large have no particular expertise in "religious" or "Islamic" issues.

If reporting on Islam is placed here in the broader context of a more comprehensive coverage of religion in journalism[1] it is to emphasise that the perception and representation of Islam are bound by fundamentally the same ethical standards as those of Christianity and the Church, or other religions such as Judaism or Buddhism.

Nevertheless, differences cannot and must not be ignored. For instance, when handling the topic of Islam a balance should always be sought between the principle of freedom of the press and free speech on the one hand, and responsibility for the consequences of a piece of journalism on the other.

1. Journalists bring professionalism to reporting on religion

A prerequisite for political journalism is a basic knowledge of political structures, and in a similar way religious journalism also requires an adequate level of expertise. A problem with this is that, because of its interdisciplinary nature

---

[1] "Religion in journalism" refers to the journalistic perception of religious themes, personalities and events, and the language of presentation. The term is therefore not restricted to journalism for which the religious communities and churches themselves are responsible.

across all news categories, religion in journalism is covered by a variety of editorial staff. This means that religious topics, personalities and events may be handled by the political, features, regional and local news desks.

Few editorial teams are able to call on a cross-departmental "church editor" with corresponding religious theological training. Not even this would solve the problem as the situation in radio stations shows: although there may well be religious broadcast programming, the managing editors generally come with a Christian theological background and their knowledge of other religions (in this instance, Islam) depends on the extent of their personal interests.

Organisationally, too, it would be difficult to envisage a "cross-departmental" editor, or a reporter with overall responsibility, because this would inevitably lead to internal demarcation disputes (for "interfering" in other editorial departments) or to excessive personal workload (offloading on to the expert by the other editorial desks all issues concerning his or her specialist area of religion, or Islam). Furthermore, it is hard to imagine that such a person would have sufficient expertise beyond their specialist area of religion to work confidently and knowledgeably for the other editorial departments (see also section 2 below).

The solution is not new or additional structures, but an atmosphere of collegial cooperation. A good and sensible idea would be to sensitise freelance editors and journalists to such issues, and to make religious reporting an integral part of training courses for journalists. The educational work of the churches and other religious organisations certainly has a greater part to play here and they should be encouraged to show a greater interest in, and commitment to, the initial and continuing training of journalists required to work in the secular media and show expertise in religious matters.

2. Journalists give a diversity of structure in language and image to topical religious themes, events and personalities

The portrayal of religion in journalism must mean more than mere factual reporting. Wherever possible, brief concise news items and reports should be complemented by explanatory comment which, in the stronger narrative format of reportage or portrait, is better suited to explaining complex religious phenomena.

The selection of pictures and their contexts requires special care because it is here that, even if without intent, clichés appear and are widely disseminated. For example, it is a particular problem for the reporting of Islam that symbols such as the minaret, the hijab or the mosque have acquired negative connotations among certain sections of the population and political activists. However typical these symbols may be, it must be considered whether their use may unintentionally deepen these negative attitudes and affect the entire report or topic, so that the reader or viewer is unable to give proper attention to the content.

At the same time, it is possible to be too timid, too considerate, for it is precisely familiarity with such symbols that ought to help the ordinary citizen – the media consumer – to break down prejudice, to bridge and overcome the divide. Misplaced timidity merely confirms that a problem exists. But it is a problem for the majority society; similar to the widespread reluctance in the media and in society to use the word "Jewish" – as if it were a term of abuse.

3. Journalists provide a multi-faceted picture of religion

It is unhelpful to make sweeping judgements about religion, not least about Islam, because this dangerously entrenches cliché and prejudice. Extremists who claim to be acting in the name of religion soon become equated with the peaceful Muslim majority. As a result the *entire* faith community is deemed to be radical, and this sows and feeds fear, mistrust, rejection and hostility.

The media should therefore intensify their efforts to provide a nuanced portrayal of individual lives – a simple farmer in Afghanistan, a Muslim Brother in Egypt, a Turkish corner store shopkeeper. Though in no way representing the Muslim community "as a whole" (any more than generalisations about Christians or Jews do), such portraits would nevertheless foster greater understanding, remove the sense of demonisation and help to normalise relations among different faith groups.

In this way the media consumer gains the insight that "the others" are not so very different; that they, too, have their cares and needs, their fears and also their faith. But of course it is important to show this faith in an everyday context, drawing parallels where possible with the faith of the reader, listener or viewer; parallels in ethics, doctrine and the lived faith.

4. Journalistic perception of religion between the poles of perception of self and perception of others

Journalistic reporting of religion is multi-layered and therefore not susceptible of simple, concise definition, nor of regulation. For some journalists it is irrelevant *which* religion is involved in the relationship and interplay between state and religion. Some focus on the relationship between different religions, while others concern themselves with *one particular* religion.

A further distinction to be made is whether the journalists in question are themselves members of the religion they are reporting on, and how important their belief is to them: a strong identification with their own religion will naturally have a different effect on their reporting than a position of greater critical distance. Of course, everyone has the right to combine faith and career, but inevitably the consequences no longer match the ideal of factual, objective reporting.

However, the expertise of staff reporters should not be overlooked, for with appropriate journalistic skills they are more skilled than clerics or religious scholars at communicating detailed knowledge about a particular religion to a broad public. On the other hand, what causes scepticism and mistrust is when a journalist is working to the brief of a particular faith community. As in other spheres of journalism the suspicion of partiality and bias then arises, which in the context of religious reporting approximates to mission.

5. Journalistic perception of religion between the poles of criticism and inclusiveness

Criticism is acceptable when justified. Problems and conflicts should not be ignored or passed over in silence out of a false sense of consideration, especially when dealing with issues of integration, or differences and arguments between Muslim immigrants and the non-Muslim majority population. This would be counterproductive to society's aim of reducing or removing barriers to integration. For journalists, but without a false "sense of mission", this represents an important – perhaps the most important – role.

However, in order to live up to both task and role, distance and objectivity must be maintained. Excessive attention to political correctness is as mistaken and harmful as excessive criticism. Journalists must find their own way founded on the principle of a free and democratic society, open to all desiring to participate in it, but defending itself against those who oppose it or wish to impose their will, from Islamic extremists to anti-Islam fanatics. Attempts to legislate for this through politics or the justice system are bound to fail. Politicians and the judiciary cannot, and should not, impose regulation, nor attempt to define the role and function of journalism.

6. The journalistic perception of religion plays an educative role, through which journalists can contribute to interreligious understanding

As in other areas of reporting, the journalistic task and function in reporting on religion are: actualities, events, processes and connections; also background information and explanatory comment. In recent years the importance of events in domestic, foreign and security affairs has been on the increase, with the relationship to Islam always at the heart of discussion. But the media perspective on other religions – in Germany, Judaism above all – plays a significant role.

The topics that give rise to reports on "Islam" or "Judaism" range widely, from Germany's past to Israeli policies today, from Islamic terrorism in distant countries to the question of, for example, Muslim religious education in German schools.

The mere fact that these themes are so topical requires the media to engage with them, but at the same time their handling of such issues can, and should, make a contribution to reducing the problems associated with them. This calls for considerable self-responsibility in the media, but it does not exclude cooperation by the religious communities and other public bodies – on the contrary, it makes it the more to be desired.

Interreligious Textbook Research and Development: A Proposal of Standards

Johannes Lähnemann

The importance of textbook research – even in the age of audio-visual media – lies in the fact that school textbooks pass on fundamental knowledge to the younger generation: selected, methodologically prepared texts (historical and religious sources, stimulus texts, material for commiting to memory), key themes, pictures, suggestions. In a situation of limited specialist training for teachers, textbooks often "teach the teachers" and play a substantial role in lesson planning.

Interreligious textbook research is of particular relevance in the face of the sweeping generalizations, prejudice and stereotypes regarding other religions and cultures ("Islam is like this" – "The West is like that") that were, and still are, to be found in school textbooks. They are not infrequently reinforced by the media and can easily be misused for political ends. In the tension between a "Clash of Civilisations" and the "Dialogue among Civilisations" that is needed, school textbooks have an important task (Hock/Lähnemann 2005, p. 394). In this respect, we look at cultures not as fixed entities. Differentiations and changes in the different beliefs and in different regions are to be taken seriously.

Based on this understanding and the experience of the research project "The representation of Christianity in textbooks of countries with an Islamic tradition" (Hock/Lähnemann 2005)[1] we propose below a set of "Standards" for interreligious school textbook development as possible guidelines for author teams and publishers, for education authorities and curriculum planners. The Standards show how interreligious issues should be handled in curriculum and textbook design.[2]

---

1   K. Hock/J. Lähnemann (Ed.): Die Darstellung des Christentums in Schulbüchern islamisch geprägter Länder. Hamburg 2005. I. W. Reiss: Ägypten und Palästina. = Pädagogische Beiträge zur Kulturbegegnung Bd. 21. II. P. Bartsch: Türkei und Iran. = Pädagogische Beiträge zur Kulturbegegnung Bd. 22. Cf. Christianity in Islamic Textbooks. Panorama 16 (2004/2005), 105-119. K. Hock/ J. Lähnemann/ W. Reiss: Schulbuchforschung im Dialog. Das Christentum in Schulbüchern islamisch geprägter Länder. Frankfurt 2006. = Beiheft der Zeitschrift für Mission 5.

2   These standards are the result of an interreligious and international process of consultation. In spite of the multiple levels recognized in this process, not all possible settings could be taken in

To achieve this we envisage issues and tasks under eight headings:

1) an authentic, professionally sound portrayal of the religions,
2) developing a dialogue orientated interpretation of religion and belief,
3) portraying the religions and their importance in the lives of real people,
4) how history is to be handled,
5) dealing with religions' cultural heritage and their contextuality,
6) the controversial issue of attitudes to the phenomenon of mission, to religious freedom and tolerance,
7) mutual understanding in the field of ethics,
8) the life conditions of the students and their relevance for religious learning and
9) pedagogical and media didactic approaches which accept the students as independent partners in the learning processes.

First we summarise the need for each heading and the tasks involved; we then describe the respective problem areas, and finally we set out the Standards to be achieved.[3]

1. Portraying the religions in an authentic, professionally sound way

1.1

Real dialogue requires that a religion should be portrayed through understanding of self rather than understanding of the other. But also a serious critical view from outside can be helpful. Distorted images and difficult prejudices can be overcome through a pedagogy that is pluralist and presents multiple views for example between an author and a practitioner of the faith. Contradictions arising between self-understanding and understanding the other should be examined and the underlying assumptions explored.

---

account. Therefore, the standards cannot directly be brought to practice. They need to be reflected regarding the specific contexts and practical conditions.

3 For positive examples in new texbooks cf. the textbook research contributions of the IXth Nuremberg Forum – in J. Lähnemann (ed.): Visionen wahr machen. Interreligiöse Bildung auf dem Prüfstand. Hamburg 2007, 490-513. Klaus Hock presents in his contribution an overview about the constructive elements in different countries with a Muslim Majority.

1.2

One problem is that religious communities have often seen themselves, or still see themselves, as competitors in the claim to exclusive truth; or they exist side by side and ignore each other. Also, textbook authors sometimes lack the training and academic qualifications necessary for a sound understanding of the different religions. Furthermore, interreligious topics are rarely given enough space within the syllabus.

1.3

For this Standard textbook authors should have access to professionally sound sources from the religions in question, backed up by reliable religious scholarship.

Care should be taken to consider the religious communities in the round; not through individual unconnected characteristics, but through their religious beliefs, fundamental views on the coherence of life, their teachings, rituals, social structures and ethics. However, differences within a religious tradition should be addressed accurately and sensitively.

Authenticity has an additional meaning: that expert adherents of each religion are actively involved in the process of correcting, supplementing, even writing. This calls for interreligious and interdisciplinary cooperation for which religious studies and educational sciences are of special relevance.

Besides this there should be professionally sound interdisciplinary collaboration, and coordination between religious education, moral education and other subjects (history, geography and social sciences, musical and language teaching …) whose textbooks touch religious content. A task of this complexity calls for a careful division of labour among the subject areas, a clear overall didactic plan reflecting current research into teaching and learning with special consideration to the continuity of learning from one age group to the next aiming at the competence to be able to deal with different world views.

2. Developing a dialogue orientated interpretation of religion and belief

2.1

An accurate presentation of the beliefs of others is only possible if the interpretation of their core teachings is based on discussion with theologians and educators of the other religions. The effort must be made to set out what is binding in the beliefs of different religions, what differs in emphasis but is not necessarily controversial, and what after all is contradictory and incompatible.

2.2

The challenge here, especially from a religious education point of view, is that there is no long tradition or experience of exchanging views on religious beliefs. This difficulty is compounded by the traditional structural relationship, especially between Judaism, Christianity and Islam, whereby younger religions cast the older in their own mould (causing thereby a sense of expropriation and misunderstanding). The older religions, meanwhile, perceive the younger to have distorted their own religious convictions. In the religions of south-east Asia, Hinduism and Buddhism are often a source of popular topics (Yoga, Dalai Lama …) but they are rarely considered in the overall context of the particular religious tradition.

2.3

Here the Standard must be to link the writing of school textbooks to the fundamental work of theological reflection in the religions as well as to religious studies research and encouragement to explore original texts.

This requires a challenging core conceptual framework for the religions in which textbook writers participate without undue obstacles to comprehension. The educational task is thus accepted as a valid component of, and is embedded in, theological and religious studies work. Interpreting the fundamental texts and traditions of other religions is a way of engaging openly with the content of other religious traditions. The aim should be to think in terms of interconnection (Karl-Josef Kuschel), not separation, nor unilateral confrontation or harmonisation. In this way what unifies, or differs in emphasis or is contradictory, becomes apparent; as do mutual influences and stimuli. To present points of view which one does not share respectfully and in their contexts is especially challenging (for example, the view of Jesus in the New Testament tradition and in the Qur'an, or the world view in Judaism, Christianity and Islam compared with Buddhism and Hinduism) (Kuschel 2007).

3. Portraying the religions and their importance in the lives of real people

3.1

Religions cannot be comprehended solely through their teachings, traditions, rituals and aesthetic forms of expression. Their true meaning lies in their impact on the lives of real, ordinary people in a variety of cultural contexts especially in the country where a textbook is to be published . (For example, how do Hindus celebrate Holi in England? What does the Sabbath mean in the everyday life of a liberal American Jew? Or of a woman who is an orthodox Israeli Jew? How do they experience the Sabbath; what interpretations from Jewish tradition are important or helpful to them?)

3.2

Many textbooks are dominated by a view of religion from an external, objective viewpoint. Even self-portrayals may adhere to a descriptive, theologically normative level. Just what impact religion actually has (which can be in tension with what it "ought to have" in the opinion of a religion's theologians and experts) on subjective experiences, on coping with life's problems, on the meaning and experience of happiness in the lives of "normal", ordinary people, is not adequately explained.

3.3

This Standard should illustrate the "Sitze im Leben" (the sociological setting) of a religion or its components through vivid, concrete examples of real, average – preferably young – people.[4] In this way individual differences can be seen, as

---

4   The principle of "personalization" can be helpful: using ideal-typical figures from other faiths in order to illuminate the different self-understandings found there, thus establishing a meeting-

well as the diversity of ways in which a religion is practised. This would counteract the difficult issue of textbooks which portray religion as a fixed and rigid structure, incapable of renewal or change.

4. Conveying a differentiated view of history

4.1

A special challenge for school textbook writers is the two-way perception of how the religions developed historically. Traditionally, textbooks have concentrated largely on the history of social tensions, selecting dates and events from the troubled periods of encounter between the religions and their political and social legacy. By contrast, the history of cross-fertilisation and cultural exchange receives scant attention, and migration can be a fascinating context for study of differences and continuities. Successful examples taken from history can inspire alternative views of the past and the present.

4.2

One's own perception of history, often associated with accusations and insinuations, frequently legitimises a sense of superiority of one religion over others. The self-identity of religious communities and denominations is often sustained by the exaggeration of historical slights and the celebration of "victories", especially where ethnic identity was, and is, part of this. In many fields a critical analysis of the historical constructions is in its infancy and far from achieving wide currency. Yet students can have a sense of being part of history, including a global dimension of history.

4.3

This Standard should allow the cultural achievements and cross-fertilisation of the religions to be duly acknowledged, without ignoring the history of conflict ("the Crusades", "the Turks at the Gates of Vienna"). For this sources should be

---

point which helps pupils to grasp what the lesson is all about. Cf. W. Haußmann: 'Walking in other People's Moccassins'? Openness to other religions in confessional religious education: possibilities and limits. BJRE Volume 13 No 2 Spring 1993.

used with great care, and views accommodate a shift in perspective (Biener 2007). Writing teams should consult historians from the religious communities as well as secular historians in order to avoid sweeping historical generalisations, too often the tinder that has ignited new conflicts. In this way a living and differentiated view of history can emerge.

5. Taking account of the cultural heritage and contextuality of the religious communities

5.1

Religions are more than a teaching edifice. They represent living greatness – with their traditions of worship, their prayers, meditations, educational and pastoral work and, not least, their aesthetic forms of expression: music, theatre, dance, and performing arts. They have shaped philosophical traditions of thought, with the result that it was the Jewish and Islamic, the Classical and Christian heritage that laid the foundations of Western civilisation.

5.2

School textbooks have hitherto – with some exceptions – largely ignored the cultural traditions of other religions. This is often due to their minority status, but also to the derogatory view taken, both historically and ideologically, of other religious communities.[5] Yet the contribution made by the different religious cultures to the social structures of individual countries is important.

5.3

For this Standard textbooks should incorporate the formative cultural and social effects of the different religions, especially of a country's own minorities. This includes perceptions of the life of faith and spiritual forms of expression and their relevance to the direction of one's life; also awareness of education and science and of social and charitable activities.

---

5   While European textbooks do at least occasionally refer to the culture of Islamic Andalusia, rarely mentioned is that of the Orthodox and Ancient Near Eastern churches.

6. Dealing openly with the topical issues of mission, tolerance and interreligious dialogue

6.1

"No peace among the nations without peace among the religions", "No peace among the religions without dialogue among the religions" – these principles formulated by Hans Küng present a huge educational challenge affecting all, including the religions, in our globalised world. Given religious claims of absolute truth and sense of mission, it cannot be taken for granted that they will come about. For a belief in mission is the premise on which religions crossed geographical boundaries. When a comprehensive message of salvation is part of religious conviction, the urge is that it should be universal. It would be dishonest to omit this from discussions of the religions. The right to bear witness to, and canvass for, one's faith is as much part of positive religious freedom as the principle that this must be without any kind of pressure or dishonest influence.

Regional and global activity among the religions includes an increase in working together for peace and social justice across religious boundaries, and evaluating this for educational purposes should follow.

6.2

In previous textbook analyses mission has proved a particularly sensitive theme in the way it is portrayed. In the Islamic world, but also on the Indian subcontinent, mission is widely (and simplifyingly) seen as the traumatic legacy of the colonial era, resulting in a negative portrayal of, and strong warnings against, Christian missionary activity. Christian cultural establishments in particular were accused of dishonest attempts to gain converts.[6]

Islam, on the other hand, has often – since its rapid expansion in early centuries – been accused of a basic aggressiveness. The fact that it can demonstrate a long history of relative tolerance and the nurture of philosophical cultural traditions was largely disregarded.

So far the history – albeit of recent date – of work towards understanding and peace among the religions has yet to be reflected in more than a few textbooks.

---

6 It should be recognised that the great missionary societies in the west have long since been pioneers of open religious dialogue, advocates for indigenous cultures and promoters, in social or educational terms, of those bodies which reject proselytising (that is, using dishonest means to convert others to one's own faith).

For this Standard, future textbooks, as well as describing the religions' different messages of salvation, should contain the history of interreligious dialogue and interreligious encounter, the groundbreaking signs and declarations.[7] There are the prayers for peace in Assisi or on Mount Hiei in Japan, the "Parliament of the World's Religions" and its Declaration Towards a Global Ethic (1993), the international movement "Religions for Peace", and last but not least, local initiatives such as meeting centres, dialogue weeks, prayers and meditations for peace. Any of these may serve as examples in school textbooks.

7. Finding common ground in ethics

7.1

That the different religions have much in common in their fundamental ethics is shown particularly clearly in the Global Ethic Project initiated by Hans Küng. At the Parliament of the World's Religions in Chicago in 1993 a declaration was signed by all major religious leaders affirming the precept of the Golden Rule ("Do unto others as you would have others do unto you") and four irrevocable directives taken from the four ethical commandments of the Decalogue and the obligations undertaken voluntarily by a lay Buddhist: non-violence, solidarity, truthfulness and partnership (Küng/Kuschel 1993). These fundamental convictions do not constitute a uniform ethic. They have to be discussed and concretised in different contexts and in exchange with non-religious humanistic positions.

7.2

The declaration for a global ethic has been studied widely from Germany to Iran but appears in only a few European textbooks. But the educational initiatives and

---

7   One measure, and not only for Christians and Muslims, was provided by the Chambésy Declaration by the World Council of Churches in 1976. This states that, "Muslims as much as Christians have an absolute right to persuade and to be persuaded, to live by their faith, and to organise their religious life in accordance with their religious duties and principles". (It was endorsed at a meeting with the World Muslim Congress in Colombo 1982). The present day dialogue is inspired by the Amman Interfaith message (http://ammanmessage.com) and the letter of 138 Muslim representatives to Christian leaders of 13.07.2007 (www.acommonword.com).

resources of the Global Ethic Foundation bear impressive testimony to how learning together in an interreligious and collaborative pedagogy can address ethical issues in a nuanced, up-to-date way.

7.3

This Standard should aim to provide school textbooks with the core ethical beliefs common to the religions – while respecting the different foundations. The declaration for a global ethic would be a helpful guide here because the ethical commandments of the Decalogue and the lay Buddhist obligations are expressed as positive aspirations. They also extend beyond the individual, addressing aspects of society, ecology and communication.[8]

8. The life conditions of the students and their relevance for religious learning

8.1

In schools as well as in society, there is no longer confessional homogeneity – not only in European countries. Children and youth are growing up in an environment which is plural in religious matters and in matters of world views. But nevertheless they all have the fundamental questions of life of which religions and world views are the predominant agents – the questions of life and death, of the central meaning of life, of justice and injustice, of overcoming sorrow and trouble. Teachers should be able to find out and recognize the situation and the questions of the students in their specific living context: What do I know about their upbringing, their experiences, needs, wishes, questions? It is a challenge for textbook writers to take this dimension seriously and to give impulses for it to the teachers.

---

8   These are the four commitments 1) to a culture of non-violence and respect for all life (not only "You shall not kill"); 2) to a culture of solidarity and a just economic order (not just "You shall not steal); 3) to a culture of tolerance and truthfulness (not just "You shall not bear false witness); 4) to a culture of partnership and equal rights between men and women (not just "You shall not commit adultery"). These directives should not be seen as a fixed codex; they should be the start for a learning process which inspires responsible action in personal as well as in social life.

8.2

In textbook tradition, it is still largely a deficit that the children's fundamental questions are mostly not taken as seriously as they should – even where intercultural education is intended. Thus the plurality as well as the individuality of the students is not properly recognized.

8.3

It should be a standard for textbooks writers to take the lead from children and adolescents with their interests, their searching for guidance, for meaning in life, belief and responsibility of behaviour. Encounter with the world of the religions should promote a culture of questioning among the students, fostering their curiosity, learning about symbols, empathy, but also their ability to think critically and with discrimination. Many of the central interpretations for life are found in the world's religions; leading figures as role models, stories, pictures, rituals and ceremonies and social activities – all are capable of vivid, stimulating presentation in textbooks. As far as possible textbooks should also deal with the "religion of children and young people"; in other words, students should be shown young people with whom they can identify.

9. Portraying religions vividly and age-appropriately

9.1

Since we began our school textbook research, the didactic and methodological potential in education of active, structured learning has aroused international interest. Only in the past ten years have these learning processes on the topic of the religions really taken off in Germany. Thirty years ago the topic was virtually confined to the final stage of the Gymnasium (upper secondary school). Now the topic is "debordered" by handling the questions according to age group, debordered through cognitive and existential activity and debordered through multiperspectivity already in the primary school. Many ideas have come from religious education practice in Great Britain which made early progress because of its long experience of cultural diversity and its non-confessional approach.

9.2

The fundamental problem here is that, to a large extent, religious socialisation in families does not exist. Even the efforts of the religious communities themselves to fill the education gap reach only a small proportion of adolescents. On the other hand, the European project "Religion in Education. A contribution to Dialogue or a factor of Conflict in transforming societies of European countries (REDCo)" has shown that young people generally are interested in finding out about religions, and that the school is best placed to provide this information. However, religious education and history teachers generally have very limited specialist skills in this area: courses are usually too short and the knowledge they provide about the religions is often superficial. This places even greater responsibility on the textbooks.

9.3

For this Standard the topic of the religions should be handled in a structured way appropriate to the age group: from simple explanations familiar to the children's own experiences to wider contexts. Equal attention should be given to the cognitive, existential and social learning outcomes. Students should be introduced to learning through encounter, an opportunity now widely available, and to the cultural manifestations and achievements of the religions. Though it is ideal if the other is an explicit interlocutor, at least textbooks make it possible to get to know the other as implicit interlocutor. Where direct conversation is not feasible, there are stories, biographies and experiences narrated first-hand.

Finally, the extra-curricular life of the school can include festivals, arts events and partnerships beyond the school itself.

School textbooks can initiate and inform, but putting the ideas into practice depends heavily on the skills of the teachers. Essential background knowledge and contexts should be clarified in authoritative teacher handbooks.

It is important that the encounter with the world of religions is open in such a way that teachers as well as students are not forced to accept a special religious viewpoint. The multiplicity of perspectives offered in the religious traditions, but also the critical view from outside should be guaranteed, and so encourage vivid, enriching and also critical learning.

In conclusion, the Standards proposed here may be regarded not only as suitable guidelines for future school textbook design for interreligious learning, but may also be applied to textbook research and the evaluation of new textbooks.

They complement the recommendations of UNESCO and the League of Arab States regarding textbook design for the teaching of history in Europe and in the Arab-Islamic world.
Last but not least, they may assist in the evaluation of other media.

References

Biener, Hansjörg (2007), *Herausforderungen zu einer multiperspektivischen Schulbucharbeit. Eine exemplarische Analyse am Beispiel der Berücksichtigung des Islam in Religions-, Ethik- und Geschichtsbüchern*, Pädagogische Beiträge zur Kulturbegegnung Bd. 25, Hamburg: EB-Verlag.

Hock, Klaus / Lähnemann, Johannes (2005), Schulbuchforschung interreligiös – auf dem Weg zu besserem gegenseitigen Verstehen, in: J. Lähnemann (ed.): *Bewahrung – Entwicklung – Versöhnung. Religiöse Erziehung in globaler Verantwortung. Referate und Ergebnisse des Nürnberger Forums 2003*, Pädagogische Beiträge zur Kulturbegegnung Bd. 23, pp. 380–398.

Hock,Klaus / Lähnemann, Johannes (ed.) (2005), *Die Darstellung des Christentums in Schulbüchern islamisch geprägter Länder*, Hamburg: EB-Verlag.

Küng, Hans / Kuschel, Karl-Josef (ed.) (1993), *A Global Ethic. The Declaration of the Parliament of the World's Religions*, London: Continuum.

Kuschel, Karl-Josef (20007), *Juden – Christen – Muslime. Herkunft und Zukunft*, Düsseldorf: Patmos.

List of Authors

Prof. Dr. Heiner **Bielefeldt**, Professor of Human Rights and its Ethics, University of Erlangen-Nuremberg, Germany, and UN Special Rapporteur on the Human Right of Religious Freedom and Belief

Prof. Dr. Saeid **Edalatnejad**, Assistant Professor at the Encyclopaedia Islamica Foundation, Tehran, Iran

Prof. Johanna **Haberer**, Professor of Christian Journalism, Vice-President of the University of Erlangen-Nuremberg, Germany

Prof. Dr. Johannes **Lähnemann**, former Professor of Religious Education at the University of Erlangen-Nuremberg, Germany; Chairman of the Peace Education Standing Commission (PESC) of "Religions for Peace" (RfP)

Rabbi Prof. Dr. Jonathan **Magonet**, former Director of the Leo Baeck Colleges of Jewish Studies, London

Dr. Daniel **Meier**, Journalist and theologian at the University of Erlangen-Nuremberg, Germany

Prof Dr. Horst **Niesyto**, Professor of Education, University of Education at Ludwigsburg, Germany

Peter **Philipp**, Journalist with leading German newspapers and radio stations, long-time correspondent in the Middle East

Prof. Dr. Manfred L. **Pirner**, Professor of Religious Education, University of Erlangen-Nuremberg, Germany

Dr. Norman **Richardson**, Head of Teaching & Learning in Religious Studies at Stranmillis University College, Belfast, Northern Ireland, and Secretary of the Northern Ireland Inter-Faith Forum

Prof. Dr. Matthias **Rohe**, Professor of Civil Law, Private International Law and Comparative Law, University of Erlangen-Nuremberg, Germany, Director of the Erlangen Center for Islam and the Law in Europe

Dr. Markus A. **Weingardt**, Researcher at the Research Institute of the Protestant Academic Association, Heidelberg, and at the World Ethos Foundation, Tübingen, Germany